FINDING LIFE
IN BETWEEN

A Journal for Me ... to You

CANDY LEIGH

ISBN: 978-1-734569-38-4

Library of Congress Control Number: 2020915689

Cover Design: Meredith Hancock, hancockmedia.com

Interior Layout & Formatting: Ronda Taylor, heartworkcreative.com

The Unapologetic Voice House
Scottsdale, AZ
www.theunapologeticvoicehouse.com

Dedication

This book is dedicated to all the women and men who are finding the courage to tell their stories and share their truths, to all who are committed to stepping into their own power to live their authentic lives.

I dedicate this book to all who are pausing, who are taking time to reflect on the scenes from their lives, who are figuring out how to savor the moments in between their own milestones.

I dedicate this book to anyone who is coping with their own dark thoughts, dark memories, or dark experiences.

This book is dedicated to anyone committed to healing through openness and conversation, to those who are doing their best to move out of survival and into thriving.

I dedicate this book to those who have hurt me, with or without intent; I am grateful for the lessons learned, and I forgive you.

I dedicate this book to those I have hurt, with or without intent, and I humbly ask your forgiveness.

I dedicate this book to the friends and angels in my life who have reminded me that life is a journey best lived with an unbridled heart and an open mind, and to those who have encouraged me to maintain a free spirit and to always look for sunshine after the rain.

I dedicate this book to every soul on a journey to peace, to all who are determined to find themselves on the open road of this crazy thing called life.

This book is dedicated to all of the Shevil Knevils, past and present, because no matter how many points are on the board at the end of the final jam, we are all winners at life. Never say die!

I dedicate this book to my three children, who have taught me grace and patience and more love than I imagined was possible. To Sydney: You are Determination. *Naguna Speena*, baby girl, you were born to fly. To Micah: You are Adventure. I love you all the way to the moon. To Camden: You are the Culmination. I love you and love you. To all three of you: Don't ever stop showing up.

Be courageous. Love yourself enough to chase the life you're dreaming of. I dedicate this book to all of you who are bravely choosing to find your life . . .in between.

Contents

FOREWORD XI

1

THE WINDING ROAD

INVITATION 1

SEMI-CHARMED AND SUN-KISSED 3

LIFE, INTERRUPTED 11

RED RIBBONS. 17

2

PACKING (AND UNPACKING) REAL LIFE

ROLLER DERBY. 25

JOLTED 31

DIVORCE. 41

ACUTE STRESS DISORDER 51

SELF-CARE JOURNALING FROM THE WOODS .57

COCO. 71

REENTRY 79

3

AUGUST ADVENTURES

FINDING YOUR TRIBE 87

AUGUST 11 97

BIG DICK ENERGY 103

CAGED BIRDS 109

HEY, MISSOURI 117

"FRAMILY" 125

PROTECT YOUR PEACE 131

COMING HOME 139

CHAPTER FOUR: MOM 143

JESSICA 147

BLIND DATE 151

4

TRAVEL NOTES

JOURNAL PROMPTS 163

AFTERWORD: TEAR OUT 167

ACKNOWLEDGMENTS 169

AUTHOR BIO 175

"A Goddess is a woman who emerges from deep within herself. She is a woman who has honestly explored her darkness and learned to celebrate her light. She is a woman who is able to fall in love with the magnificent possibilities within her. She is a woman who knows of the magic and mysterious places inside her, the sacred places that can nurture her soul and make her whole. She is a woman who radiates light. She is magnetic."

—UNKNOWN

FOREWORD

⇥

As I write this, "in these uncertain times" is a phrase used to discuss the COVID-19 world health pandemic, the status of our economy, the stock market, our personal health, and so much more. It elicits panic for some and light caution for others while some don't seem to be bothered at all. It causes some to look at their financial accounts with increasing concern while others hold their loved ones close and hope and pray an invisible illness doesn't steal their family members away. Others think this virus to be a hoax and refuse to acknowledge science.

While our traditional lives have been turned upside down by this pandemic, we have also been given a unique opportunity to pause, to slow down. This virus has forced us to step back into our lives and our homes in a more intentional way. It has given us an opportunity to assess our current lifestyles and assumptions, and it has prompted us to perhaps not take certain relationships and life events for granted.

In many ways, times of uncertainty in my life inspired the chapters of this book. The stories contained within these pages were born of journeys that weren't planned and weren't orchestrated. Rather, the stories organically unfolded as life actually happened, in between the planned (and once-taken-for-granted) milestones, when nothing was certain yet everything was possible.

As I reflect on my life's journey, I honor the knowledge I've gained as well as the lessons I realize I have yet to learn. There is much more to see and do and experience. Even so, I know I have much to share. My belief is that when we share our humanity through authentic stories, we open ourselves to the opportunity to transform and heal. This book is a part of my healing. Perhaps it will be a part of yours.

As you read these pages, I encourage you to remember your own stories, not just the milestone moments documented by pictures planned and posed but the moments in between point A and point B, where the only photos that exist are the ones etched in your heart. Examine your own moments of clarity, of craziness, of wisdom. Reflect on your own emotions and how you have personally navigated those profound liminal spaces in between the peaks and valleys of life. Think about how you've survived your journey, what's really gone on behind the scenes of your social media highlights, and who has been there to celebrate and commiserate with you along the way. Get real with yourself about life's biggest triumphs and life's biggest traumas. Remember to build, or imagine building, resilience because the muscle of resilience is what we need to flex when, inevitably, we encounter uncertain times and we have to pivot, and pivot, and maybe pivot again.

In these uncertain times, our real-life stories are more important than ever. Life is now divided by an unexpected milestone, time now known as pre- and post-pandemic. How we choose to survive will include making moves according to a script that is yet unwritten. We are living in the "in between times," the transition between what was and what will be, the dash that ties together our beginning and end. In these uncertain times, our stories are what will guide us into our new normal and our new sense of reality.

Once told, our stories will have the power to create a consciously connected family across time and distance. When we choose to share our voices and journeys, we all rise, we all heal, and we all learn to love ourselves—and each other—a little more.

As you read, I hope you are inspired to savor the authentic moments of real life that make up the entire continuum of your personal journey. I hope you choose to celebrate *Finding Life In Between*.

CONTENT WARNING: *Topics explored in this book may be unsettling for some. All are encouraged to read only if and when it is the right time and right choice for that individual. Topics within the pages include but are not limited to mental illness/depression, loss, death of a pet, abuse, assault, rape, theft, language, racism, and divorce. Topics also include gratitude, travel, hope, healing, personal growth, friendship, inspiration, and love.*

1

THE WINDING ROAD

---

*Sometimes you turn around to look back
at the path of your life only to realize that,
actually, your journey is your destination.*

Invitation

Dear sister,

I began this journey by looking outward. I decided to combine the magic of the things I love—adventuring, traveling, connecting with people, and writing—in order to tell stories of the human experience. From the beginning, I committed to falling in love with this process, this art, this exploration of the unknown, even if it exhausted and confounded me. My goal was to dive into the spirit of human relationships and tell the tales of our connectedness, of our similarities and our differences. I was going to call my book *Unwritten ... Previously Untold Stories Collected on the Open Road.* I romanticized the idea. I was excited. I was optimistic. It felt safe to write the stories of others. I didn't know exactly how it would come together, but I could feel in my soul that it was the right journey at the right time.

Well, the right journey at the right time actually became an unexpected voyage of intense self-reflection. Rather than examining others, I was repeatedly nudged to look inward, to review the path of my own existence. The magic of traveling to unknown places along with the voices of my spirit guides and the light of the moon, led me to hear stories that opened me up to my own vulnerability. As the safety of looking outward dissipated, I was left with the fear of confronting my own experiences and beliefs. The magic that moved me led me to breathe life into words that came from my heart, through my fingers, and onto paper—the words that now fill the pages of this book. What I didn't realize was that these chapters would be my own catharsis and my own cleansing. My sister, I wanted to write for you about the stories of others, but it turned out that I needed my words for me first.

I set out to write about the spirit of human connection, a collection of short stories, celebrating the beauty of relationships and the mysteries of life. The Universe, however, decided to challenge my idea by inspiring something different—a memoir, a sort of journal about some very real experiences of modern womanhood. I decided to let go of my expectations. I sat with the uncertainty that comes when inspiration meets creativity, and now, after a great deal of fear and worry and internal debate, I've decided to gift the end result, this book, to you. I now invite you to join me on this journey of hope and healing.

The chapters within these pages are personal. They include adventures and secrets and friendships and wishes. They tell tales of conversations and connections that occured not only while traveling, but also remembering. They also share stories that I was once too afraid and too ashamed to share. Dear sister, I need you to know that as you read, I do not expect you to take responsibility for my words, and I certainly do not expect you to take on the weight of my experiences. However, I anticipate that you may find some piece of yourself within these stories, and my hope is that you decide to open yourself up to the vulnerability that might meet you in your own reflections.

Our stories alone do not define us, but they do have power. They have the power to either elevate or suffocate. My sister, I hope that, as you read, you release the burden of anything you have privately carried, and you choose to soar. I hope you choose to breathe in the life force of authenticity and the power of vulnerability. I hope you feel the magic of our connection, and I hope you know in your heart that you are not alone.

With light and love,

Candy Leigh

Semi-Charmed And Sun-Kissed

➤———→

"You walk around like you have this semi-charmed, sun-kissed life," my colleague and friend said to me as we were going back to our desks after lunch on a snowy and cold February afternoon. I was caught off guard so I hardly heard her next sentence. "No one would know you've had struggles."

I paused. Was that a backhanded compliment? I sucked in my breath. I was stuck on the other words she had used.

Semi-charmed?

Sun-kissed?

First, we were in Wisconsin in the dead gray of winter with wind chills well below zero. We were far from a "sun-kissed" anything. Second, I was surprised this was what she thought of me. It made me wonder if this was the impression that others had of me as well. I couldn't help but feel a little defensive. I had put my vulnerability on display during our lunch conversation. I trusted her. I had just told her some things that were heavy on my heart. Was she simply dismissing my struggles? Who doesn't have struggles? My struggles didn't seem to add up to what she believed was the threshold of struggling. As we walked together it now seemed that *her* perception trumped *my* reality. We walked back to our desks and made small talk.

I kept thinking, *You don't even really* know *me. You have no idea what I've been through. What I just told you was the tip of the iceberg.*

3

And you think I've led a semi-charmed and sun-kissed life? I decided not to share anything personal with her ever again.

This brief interaction forever changed how I experience people. It made me more deeply understand how very little we actually know about each other beyond the surface of what we choose to share. Everyone has a story just waiting to be told, but so many of those stories go untold and unwritten. From that point forward, not only did my conversations change, so did my perceptions of people. I tried to listen more deeply to what my friends chose to share. I tried to dig more deeply when I worked with clients. It informed my consulting work. I opened every interview with a specific and open-ended question to begin the conversation: "What's your story? How did you get here, to this point, today?"

The way people consistently responded to that opening initially surprised me, but then became predictable like the steps in a well-rehearsed waltz. First a small smile, eyes drifting slightly to the side as if replaying their favorite scenes from the reels of professional life, then, sitting back in the chair, shoulders relaxing and with a deep breath, the interviewee would share the journey of how they arrived at today. There was always, without fail, some commonality between the story shared and my own personal journey, and we could usually create an authentic bond over our connection. That bond directly and positively impacted the course of our entire conversation and, ultimately, our work together.

One such interview not only impacted but actually altered the course of my life. I was in New York for an organizational design consulting project for a financial services firm. I had just finished an hour-long conversation with the office manager. She was probably in her late twenties or early thirties, she was tall, and she wore a white pantsuit. She had long, unruly, wavy auburn hair, and she wore black-framed glasses that sat slightly down her nose. I stood up to shake her hand and end our interaction, but she didn't get up. Instead, she leaned back in her chair, folded her arms, and looked me up and down. I was immediately a bit uncomfortable. I looked at her. She looked back at me.

Silence.

Finally, she said quite matter-of-factly, "I think you could do it."

I did a double take. I was still standing and she was still sitting, contemplating me, twisting the chair from side to side. "Excuse me?" I asked. I was lost. I fidgeted nervously with my hands. "Do what?" I felt under the microscope at this point so I straightened up to look taller and hold my ground. She seemed amused by my instinctive nonverbal defensive stance.

"Roller derby," she replied, smiling, "you've got the build for it."

We both stared at each other. She was smiling, amused. I was just confused. Now this was unexpected. All of a sudden the tables were completely turned. I smiled. I sat back down. "Roller derby. Tell me more." It was the end of the day and technically I was supposed to leave the office, but instead the next hour became an entirely different conversation, and we achieved a completely different area of common ground. When I got back to my hotel that night, I googled "roller derby" and "WFTDA," which stands for Women's Flat Track Derby Association. I soaked it in. A few weeks later I signed up for tryouts for the Brewcity Bruisers, and within the next twelve months, I was officially a rollergirl.

As it turns out, that saying "you're only one decision away from having a completely different life" is actually true. That single conversation created massive change for me. Roller derby introduced me to friends I never would have met, inspired confidence I had all but lost, and reminded me that there was an entire world out there that I had yet to discover. In the course of a single conversation, one woman influenced that change. I began to wonder about all of the coaching and consulting conversations I was a part of, and I decided to be more intentional about these dialogues and how they just might be a catalyst for opportunity and personal growth.

In all of my twenty-year Fortune 500 career, the authentic conversations that came out of people sharing their stories were the ones I treasured most. In those conversations, people let down their guard and showed up and fully shared who they really were. Whether with colleagues, clients, or friends, being trusted enough for people to share their dreams, their ideas, and their vulnerabilities has always been the most rewarding aspect of my job. Why? Perhaps because the things about us that oftentimes remain untold are the things that make us most connected.

Most of us don't always present the truest versions of ourselves to the world. We leave people to form their own opinions without fully knowing who we are. This isn't necessarily a bad thing. After all, going around openly professing one's deepest secrets to strangers might also result in people forming opinions that may not be as benign as having a life that's simply "semi-charmed" or "sun-kissed." But there is something to be said for feeling connected enough to share your story freely, without judgment and without fear. When we can share our stories and create connections with others, a space within us opens up, oftentimes for healing. Through that healing, we gain a greater sense of love for ourselves and for others.

In a world that can be excruciatingly brutal, we all need healing. Even if we don't always outwardly show our vulnerabilities, we all need unconditional love. There is no such thing as too much love.

This idea of connection and healing through storytelling isn't new. Storytellers have historically played important roles in various cultures across time. Today, storytelling almost seems a bit of a lost art. I considered this as I reflected. What stories am I telling myself? What stories am I telling others? What stories are others telling about me? That last one sent me on a downward spiral. The fear of what people say behind my back is enough to send me under the covers for days, but I'm trying to love myself through that. More importantly, what stories would my kids tell about me and our family? What stories will they pass down to their kids in the future?

Our stories physically show up differently than they did years ago. Paper is no longer a necessity and communicating in person is not always feasible. We are busy connecting online, through social media, through e-mails and other electronic platforms. While some of these outlets enable us to be connected in ways we never have been, they also have had the unintended consequence of disconnecting us in profound ways. Have you ever lain in bed with your partner while one—or both of you—is on your phone rather than sharing the intimate details of your day? I can't tell you how many times I've e-mailed the person in the cubicle next to me instead of simply having a conversation. It raises a few questions: What opportunities are we missing out on when we choose to engage through technology rather than create a human/soul connection with another person? What stories are we not creating *together*? And as a result of that, what healing are we preventing from occurring, both within our own selves and in others?

These questions stirred me like I hadn't been stirred in quite a while. That stirring, I knew, meant a call to action. So I sat with my palms open, looked skyward, and meditated, *All right, Goddess, I'm listening. What do I need to learn, and what will you have me do?*

From that point forward, the puzzle pieces began to converge to reveal a picture I have yet to fully comprehend. It became clear to me that I needed to align my skills and my passions and embark on a journey of human/soul connections and storytelling. The culmination of that work is the book you have in your hands right now. Intuitively I was drawn to this space where we can share our stories and stand in our truth so that we can learn from each other, understand, heal, and love.

It was about this time in my realization that I was thrown a real curveball. I found out I was about to be laid off from my corporate job, the one with the steady paycheck and the retirement benefits and the annual bonus, the one that enables me to pay all the bills associated with running a single-income household, the one that provides health insurance for my athletic kids who break bones every year and the one kid with a life-threatening food allergy, the job that has a generous scholarship program for the kids of employees (and college is just on the horizon), you know, the job to which I gave all of my blood, sweat, and tears for the last twenty years.

I didn't know what I was going to do. How does a person survive a layoff with three kids and a mortgage and debts and a passion for living life? I was angry and I was sad and I was scared.

And for the first time in twenty years, I was about to be free.

Job loss itself is a big deal, not to mention the complexities and expenses that go with a job loss in our capitalist system. (We should all ask more questions about why it is so important that health care is tied to employment.) I don't have a partner who will cover the mortgage or pick up private health insurance for the family, and a disruption like this requires a legal change of circumstances that will impact child support, which may or may not go as smoothly as one would hope. The stress of having to deal with the legal situation alone is incredibly unnerving. But, conversely, there's something emotionally liberating when you're free from having to go into a workplace that doesn't fully value you and your story.

In those days between finding out about my layoff and actually separating from my career, I experienced every possible emotion. I gave myself permission to pause and soak in all of the madness. What I do know to be true is that *every* emotion had a purpose: the fear, the anger, the frustration, the gratitude, the elation, the sadness, the anxiety ... the everything. All those emotions needed to cycle through for me to continue on my journey. I needed to learn the life lessons of those emotions so that I could move on to my next chapter.

This learning is soul work. This is part of my story and part of my in between. Those emotions are my healing.

My emotional roller coaster and newly unemployed status thrust me into a new life chapter where the pages were incredibly blank. And scary. Those blank pages became a catalyst. They inspired me to take an inventory of my passions and my values and my *value*. I had some heart-to-heart conversations with a few trusted friends and colleagues, and I spent time reflecting on my strengths and my goals. As I sat with the quiet of my mind, my soul began to open up, and the idea for this book came alive. The idea of connecting through stories started as a flame but then became a raging fire. I wanted to travel and I wanted to move away from what seemed like a routine life. I wanted to talk with strangers and ask them about their stories and what brought them to this point, today. I wondered if I could write down the stories that I heard, so that we could all somehow find ourselves within them. I wondered if those shared stories could create space for healing for all who read them. After all, for the first time in two decades, I had no Monday morning eight a.m. commitment, and I had no place to go but everywhere.

That's when it hit me: This was *crazy*. Who in the world leaves on a road trip with no exact destination and interviews strangers to tell their stories? That sounded absolutely insane. And wonderful. Actually, my Sagittarius soul *loved* the idea. I spent one late night mapping out a road trip from southeastern Wisconsin to the Myrtle Beach area, hoping to stop to visit some friends along the way. I researched the potential route and found some random and incredible off-the-beaten-path landmarks that seemed to warrant a stop. I decided I would somehow know whom to talk to when I saw them. I planned to write down those experiences and reflections, and maybe somehow, through a compilation of all these stories and adventures, create real-life human connections.

Then it hit me all over again. This idea was absolutely nuts. Who in their right mind does something like this?

Unequivocally and with absolute certainty, I answered myself: *I do.*

Once I made that decision in my heart, the Universe conspired to make it so. The pathway began to unfold in ways I'm still trying to understand. My girlfriend told me to talk to a mutual friend who told me I had to meet her friend, so she facilitated an introduction. That new friend became the publisher of this book. A different friend introduced me to another friend (via text) who referred me to an acupuncturist who, upon hearing about my ideas for this adventure, referred me to Peggy, a Native American healer, who shared parts of her amazing story and then performed a healing on me in preparation for my journey. I read books that resonated with me and called me to create these connections and listen to people's stories. I had dinner with two incredibly talented colleagues who agreed to help me by providing their unbridled expertise and feedback. I spoke with yet another dear friend (who is an author, speaker, and coach) who talked with me about how the Universe right now is opening up this window for me to do meaningful and valuable work that speaks to my heart and my values system. She reinforced that this effort will undoubtedly positively impact others. She laughed when she reminded me in no uncertain terms that none of this would have happened if I hadn't been laid off from my super secure, comfortable, reliable (yet incredibly boring and relentless) job of twenty years.

Whoa. Gratitude.

I guess, right in that moment and under the summer sun, my life *was* a little bit semi-charmed and sun-kissed. It was, after all, August in Wisconsin, the sun was shining, the road was calling, and there were real-life stories that needed to be told.

My original loose itinerary for the month included a canoe trip, some family time, and my road trip book-writing experience. I expected to have adventures, meet people, collect their stories, and share them in the pages of this book. The conversations I had and the stories I found were sometimes short and friendly, and other times deeply passionate. But during this time, other stories, including my own, found me.

In the space between Wisconsin and the Carolinas and back again, there was reflection. There was exploration. There was magic. That magic is what I've attempted to capture on these pages in the organic way that life unfolds in all of its beautiful imperfection.

And perhaps some of this real life journey truly is semi-charmed and sun-kissed.

Life, Interrupted

⟶

believe one of the biggest lessons we all have to learn is that life's journey rarely unfolds as we expect it. We are told in our youth that anything is possible, that we should dream big, that we can be whatever we want. But as it turns out, the path from A to B is long and winding, and the detours we encounter on the journey take us in a host of directions that we often don't understand. We look forward to celebrating our arrival at life's major milestones without learning to fully embrace the journey. This is exactly what I was discussing with my friend over lunch on that aforementioned winter day. What I had expected in my life had been overturned by circumstances and choices, and many of the former were not under my own control. My life plan had been interrupted over and over again, and what I was experiencing as mere survival she perceived as thriving. I was trying to sort out the lessons within the stories, but I wasn't there yet. I'm still learning.

In one conversation I had leading up to my big road trip south, my girlfriend and I spoke about the picture of life we had created in our minds. I explained I never thought I'd be laid off from the company I loved. She was in the middle of her divorce and talking about her misconceptions about married life. Our dramatized portrayal of married life went something like this:

I always imagined life in a cute little house, and it's always clean! There's a fenced yard and a sweet cuddly dog. I have my kids at home with me during the day and we play games and they nap on schedule and eat organic food that I prepare. When my husband comes home from work he's always happy to see me and we talk together about how the day went. Dinner is ready on time and we eat as a whole family, then we clean up the kitchen together and watch TV or play a game. After the kids go to bed (without complaint) my husband and I talk about the day, make love, and go to bed in each other's arms, ready to do it all again tomorrow.

This is the stuff of fantasies and social media reels, where everything is perfect and we share only what we want others to see—semi-charmed and sun-kissed.

We laughed about our hopes and dreams versus our respective realities, which often looked more like this:

We've lived in our house for two years and the central air just went out. It's hot as fuck outside, and I can hardly take it. The fence panels need to be fixed because last winter one blew down and I don't know how the hell to fix it and my husband is never home because he's always working overtime. I'm with my kids all day every day (I love them, but I need a break!) and if I hear about Peppa Pig *or* Paw Patrol *one more time I'm seriously going to lose my shit. Speaking of shit, the dog won't stop crapping in the living room and I've had it. No one eats what I cook and I don't know why I even bother anymore! When my husband gets home from work I'm lucky if I get a shower in, and usually he's upset about his boss so I don't bother to ask him how his day went anymore, but it sounds like his new secretary, Lindi, is pretty nice. We're behind on bills so I'm thinking about picking up a part-time job but that would cut into family time, which doesn't even happen anymore, and I can't even remember the last time we actually had a date night! If we do go to bed together there certainly isn't any love-making. He smells like garlic and sweat and I'm too exhausted to even think about foreplay! I don't know how we're going to survive. How do couples make it? Does it ever get any better?*

The frustration is real. The violation of our expectations is raw. Living in survival mode is painful. As we talked we began to realize what we already knew. Life is shit. It's all about how you deal with it. And it's about finding someone who can move with you from shitstorm to shitstorm and will take turns holding the fucking umbrella.

As a student of human behavior and avid people watcher, I've been appreciating this lesson more and more as I see it play out in real time. I'm a member of an online group of divorced/divorcing women who have kids. The forum has become a place to build friendships, joke around, coordinate events, share memes, and also discuss real-life experiences of divorce, co-parenting, and dating. Some women are earlier in their divorce and co-parenting journeys, and some are more experienced in their mothering and post-divorce years. As a certified mediator and someone who has experienced the family court system, I sometimes offer an ear for a phone call, and I often share the perspective of "what really happens" during a court hearing or a Guardian ad Litem meeting.

In addition to these online friendships, I also have face-to-face friends who have gone through/are going through divorces, and the situations and emotions across the board are remarkably similar. Their experiences are painful and each individual feels the full gamut of emotions until, ultimately, their issues are somehow resolved. Divorce isn't what any of them planned when they got married and/or had kids, but it's where the road of life led. One of the major life lessons on that bumpy road is that the only thing each person can control is his or her own actions in response to whatever situation life has handed them.

My divorce was brutal. I was convinced I had failed at life. I was convinced I had ruined my kids. I was convinced that I might not survive. I didn't know how to endure the darkness of the transition from married to divorced.

In introductory communication theory classes, we discuss the downward spiral of communication—basically that negative begets negative and sends you spiraling downward. This is true of *intra*personal communication (internal dialogue) as well as *inter*personal communication (external conversation between two or more individuals). Even though I knew and had actually taught classes about the downward spiral, I found myself in this pattern during and following my divorce. I told myself I was unworthy and unlovable, that I was a sinner. I was told all I'd ever be was a part-time mom, and even though I knew that wasn't really true, I internalized the sense of sadness and loss of that idea. I believed I didn't fit in with my own family or my own community any longer.

These scary, dark and limiting thoughts can have a significant impact on your day-to-day life. But once they're out there and you name them, you can invite your fears to the table and have a conversation to do the work to eradicate them. There's messy and emotional work in reprogramming the mind, but moving from fear to freedom is important, soul-healing work. It's been said that either you're hurting or you're healing. There is honor in doing the work of healing so that your hurt doesn't become embedded and passed on to your children and the following generations.

As my children have grown into young adults, I've tried to, albeit imperfectly, focus on healing, and one of my major life lessons is my periodic need to excuse myself from daily life in order to regain perspective. This has manifested in staying the night or the weekend at a friend's house and in taking myself off the grid and into the woods for a weekend. It's taken the shape of me driving across the country or flying over the ocean to spend some time in my own thoughts before visiting people I know and love. This has given me the ability to maintain a freedom mindset, and that mindset helps me to navigate the inevitable interruptions between life's milestones. It helps me find purpose in the journey.

I am far from an expert or a test case in emotional healing and enlightenment, but I do believe that there is wisdom to be shared from our collective experiences and attempts at healing. Through real-life discussions about major life changes, we can learn to appreciate our truths without sugarcoating certain things and keeping other things secret. Our plans for our lives will undoubtedly be riddled with interruptions. If we can share our real life experiences, we can better navigate those interruptions with grace, and move forward to stand in power in authenticity and truth.

Red Ribbons

➤⟶

I was face down on the table at my acupuncturist. I described to her the concept for this book while she needled my back. "I'm not sure how it will work and I don't exactly know how it will come together, but what I do know is that I *need* to do this. I need to go. I need to talk to people about what we know and what we believe because when we start to tell each other what's in our souls, something changes. We all change."

She paused for a moment to consider what I had said, then she told me that she loved the idea. I was relieved, because I was pretty sure I was crazy. Then she told me that I needed to speak to Peggy, who was visiting from Louisiana. I had no idea who Peggy was, but I told her I would be happy to meet Peggy if she had the time. When my acupuncture session was finished, I walked into the lobby to await Peggy's arrival. Usually, I'm in a rush to move from meeting to meeting, appointment to appointment, errand to home and back to do it all over again. Now, since I no longer had a corporate job and didn't have to be back at my desk at a certain time, I was consciously doing things differently. I sat patiently in the waiting area, closed my eyes and breathed deeply, and tried to soak in the sounds and smells of the room.

When Peggy walked into the lobby to meet me, her peaceful energy greeted me before she did. She stood about five foot four, yet she seemed incredibly tall. Her hair was long and dark with a few gray strands highlighting the wisdom in her face. As she approached me, her warm smile invited me into a conversation that our hearts seemed to already have started. Peggy is a Native American healer, and she only spends a portion of her summer in Milwaukee. I was actually quite lucky to meet her.

Even though I was already relaxed from my acupuncture session, I somehow felt even calmer in Peggy's presence. She took my hands in hers. She told me it was her pleasure to meet me. I told her the pleasure was mine. I shared with her a little of my story and the concept of the book, and her eyes widened. She seemed immediately taken with the idea. We sat down to talk more.

We touched on the fact that all people have gifts, and that storytelling is a treasured gift that many of our ancestors had. Their stories brought us to where we are today. We discussed how storytelling today is a bit of a lost art. As we talked, the stories we shared began to fill up the space in between us. At one point, Peggy spoke of the dark and the light inside her, and about how throughout her life's journey there were times when the dark seemed to take over, and there were times when the light seemed to win. When the darkness was wrestling and winning, it made her wonder about her own value and self-worth. She questioned whether she deserved to walk the earth. Then at other times, and with practiced meditation, the light grew stronger and overcame the darkness so that she could live peacefully within her own soul. I understood this all too well.

During my darkest days following my divorce, I often lay in the dark stillness of my room, alone, wondering if the people in my world would be better served if I didn't wake up the next morning. I imagined that their lives would go on so much more smoothly without me. But then, usually after sleep and along with the rising of the sun, a bit of light would creep into my mind and dispel the darkness, and eventually the light would begin to take hold. In these brief moments Peggy and I shared, it was as if she, in her own darkness, had already experienced a piece of me, and I, in the rebirth of the light, had already experienced a piece of her. It's maddening to realize that many of us have shared that same kind of isolating pain and struggle for emotional survival, and at the same time it's refreshing to know that it is possible to survive the pain, find the light, and overcome.

Eventually our conversation turned to my pending road trip, and I shared my thoughts on how my ideas might actually come together. I told her my thoughts about "the red ribbon."

I explained that I believe we all have a red ribbon that binds us through our hearts and our souls, and that we need to tell our stories in order to keep the ribbon from breaking. I told her that all of my thoughts on this calling and this journey were like a puzzle, and I was flipping over different pieces and arranging them to bring the entire picture into focus, but I had yet to see it fully. Peggy closed her eyes and responded in her gentle, Southern voice, "The picture is a braid being woven together, and one of the strands is that red ribbon, and it is being made stronger in the braid. When we share our stories, we weave ourselves together. We become stronger. There is a piece of me inside you, and you in me, and so it is with every one of us." She went on to say that, especially as women, we all need to be able to tell our stories and connect with others so that we can open our arms wide and truly come home to ourselves.

Come home to ourselves.

In that exact moment, time stopped, and tears immediately spilled out of my eyes. I inhaled sharply. How many of us wrestle with not only accepting but also loving our truest authentic selves? How much time over a lifetime do we spend discounting and disliking ourselves instead of celebrating and growing confident in our uniqueness? Why is it so hard to simply exist as who we are meant to be? Peggy understood and she framed it perfectly. Our journeys home to ourselves can be long and difficult, but the destination is worthy. It's one worth waking up and fighting for every single day. In these words and moments, Peggy's ribbons and my ribbons began to weave themselves together into a bond of loving respect and admiration.

A few days earlier, I visited a palm reader while wandering the crowds and tents at a summer music festival. The woman, without knowing who I was, told me that I was an artist, but not a painter, but rather an artist with words, and that I should follow that passion. The palm reader also told me that I had a very clear and bright aura surrounding my upper being, but that my lower being had a dark energy that needed a full spiritual cleansing. Once she saw I was intrigued, the palm reader told me she would promptly handle that cleansing for $250. Since I was just laid off, and because I was at a summer festival, I politely declined her offer. I told Peggy of this interaction and asked if she would be willing to help me with the cleansing. She agreed. I set an appointment for a few weeks later, right before she left to return to Louisiana, right before I left on my road trip.

The healing itself was an incredibly powerful experience. It involved meditation, spoken words, snakeskin, and energy flow. During the healing, Peggy asked me to clear my fears and give them up. There were two specific fears that I focused on. One was my fear of financial devastation. The other was the fear of never truly opening my heart to find love. Peggy understood. She directed me to focus on releasing all of my fears around those two items, and to consciously clear any thoughts that were even remotely affiliated with those fears. After the clearing, Peggy spoke words of light and love, and she called on the ancestors of all beings to guide me on my journey, to protect me and my car, and to bring me back home safely after discovering all that I was intended to find. The grace and the love that she poured into me through this healing was not only spiritual and magical, it was tangible. I could feel her energy move through me as she spoke, and again I was moved to tears. My tears came up from my heart and my soul and poured over my cheeks and spilled on the table beneath me.

At the end of the healing, Peggy wrapped my hands in hers and she asked me how I felt. "So incredibly grateful," I answered. We talked more about the framework for my upcoming travels and how my soul needed to wander away from my day-to-day routine in order to regain perspective on this life. She seemed to understand that I needed that time to make sure that the light inside me stayed strong. Peggy smiled her warm smile and told me that I was inspiring her to live with adventure. I thought, *I'm inspiring you?* This idea triggered even more emotion. She sensed it, and she squeezed my hands. Peggy asked me to stay in touch, and I assured her that I would. As tears of gratitude continued to spill onto my cheeks, I looked down at our hands, mine in hers and hers in mine, somehow looking more like they all belonged to the same being rather than two individuals. I swear I could see a red ribbon wrapped around our hands and wrists, inexplicably binding us perfectly together.

As I composed myself and Peggy wrapped up her healing tools and placed them gently back into her bag, she said to me that if, as I was driving, there was a pesky fly in the car, I shouldn't brush it away too quickly. She told me that I should let it linger, because it would be her spirit, traveling with me, so we could share a bit of the adventure together.

2

Packing (and Unpacking) Real Life

"One day you will tell your story of how you've overcome what you're going through now, and it will become part of someone else's survival guide."

—UNKNOWN

Roller Derby

→

Spending time with like-minded people who genuinely lift you up and make you shine brighter is, in itself, an act of self-care. Yet sometimes, amidst the craziness of life, we deprioritize connecting with friends and, because of that, we miss out on learning their journeys and hearing their stories. After getting restructured out of my career, time opened up for me to connect with others, and I spent time with one friend who had gone on an African excursion to climb Mt. Kilimanjaro. I also spoke to another who talked to me about the time she went on a solo hiking/camping trip to emotionally process her divorce. My Facebook memories just reminded me of a time when three girlfriends and I traveled to Puerto Rico for a long weekend of sunshine and exploring. I try to make it to both England and Arizona at least once a year to be away from the day-to-day monotony of life, and also to simply breathe the same air as people who are energetically amazing to be around. Many of these like-minded adventuring souls are people I met in roller derby.

I will never forget the thrill of watching roller derby live for the first time. It was shortly after the woman in the New York office introduced me to the fact that modern-day roller derby even existed. I watched as these women brutally handed each other their asses over and over and over again. The falls were wicked. The speed was intense. The crowd was so into it, and the rollergirls were into the crowd, sometimes literally. What struck me most was that these women oozed confidence. It made me remember what it was like to be an athlete. It made me want to be on a team again. I wanted that same confidence. I wanted that camaraderie. I was hungry for it.

I leaned over, my eyes not leaving the track, and said to my (now ex) husband, "I could do this."

He looked over at me, kind of laughed, and said, "Yeah right."

I responded, "Look, I used to be a total rink rat. I used to practice running on my toe stops so I could win free sodas at the races on Tuesday and Friday nights. I'm telling you I could do this." I heard the urgency in my voice, not sure if I was trying to convince him or convince myself. I wasn't sure if I was asking for permission or speaking my future or something in between all of that. He just kept shaking his head at me, doubting me.

Fuck that. I decided. *I'm doing it.*

In the movie *Whip It*, which we had watched in preparation for our roller derby date, one character says, "Sometimes you have to be your own hero." That's exactly how I felt.

As the bout went on, I kept hearing his doubt. What was worse, I could feel it. It made me angry. It maybe made me irrationally angry. I felt the heat rise up inside me.

Don't think I can do it? Fucking watch me. I can do anything I put my mind to. I will be my own damn hero.

The next day I went to the local skate shop and got a pair of skates, all the required gear, and I signed up for the "Fresh Brew" training and recruitment sessions. I was doing it.

Our class was one of the largest and most dedicated that the league had ever seen. I don't know how many people signed up and got started, but draft day saw about two dozen rookies placed on four different home teams. Getting drafted to a team is like Christmas. You're the gift to the team, the team is the gift to you, you get a swag bag of merch to welcome you, and pretty much everyone drinks and celebrates. Just for fun, one of your new derby sisters might slam one too many beers and get drunk and pee her pants. (True story.)

I was shaking when it was my turn to be called up. I was nervous and excited and scared and hopeful. They announced my name; I was drafted to the Shevil Knevils. I couldn't believe it. The women on that team were some of my favorite skaters! One of the skaters I admired the most from my first night of watching derby was one of my captains. When I walked into the collective arms of the team for the first time as an official Shevil, my new captain herself told me that they wanted me on the team. *They wanted me!* It felt so good to be wanted.

After all the draft announcements were made and the rookies (fresh meat) all knew the colors they'd be wearing for the season, our captains rounded up the new Shevils for a celebratory shot. When the one captain asked what I'd have, I told her I'd take a lemon drop. She looked at me with a sideways smile and slapped me on the back and said, "Well, you're a Shevil now, and we drink whiskey," and then to the bartender, "We'll take Jameson over here!"

Honestly, I didn't even know what Jameson was at that point. That was my very first shot of whiskey and became my shot of choice for as long as I wore the red, white, and blue for our home team. We practiced for two hours every Wednesday night, and we scrimmaged for two hours on Sundays, and there were cross-training practices on Saturdays, and interleague practices on Mondays. After those first few weeks of skating, my legs burned with a fire I had never known ... but my thighs looked better than when I was a teenager. Skating gave me a reason to work hard, train hard, play hard, and it brought me into a crazy and incredible sisterhood that I didn't even realize I needed.

Funny how life can bring you exactly what you need when you don't know you need it.

By the time I was skating with the Shevils my divorce was well underway. There were a lot of us in the league who were in some type of relationship transition and trying to find our path forward: some major breakups and divorces, some redefining their whole person-hood, some marriages, etc. Sometimes we discussed it, sometimes we didn't talk about it at all. But one thing was certain, you could bring all your pain and frustration and hurt and sadness into the practice space with you, and you could leave everything out on the track. There's a saying, "Roller derby saved my soul," which I believe evolves into something intensely personal for all skaters. What I know for certain is that it taught me that I actually do have the power inside me to get back up every time I get knocked down. And, as we often say, "It's better to get knocked down than get knocked up!"

One night at practice there was a skater who was also going through a divorce who took some big hits. On the last hit she stayed down, in tears. As we stopped the play to make sure she was okay, she sat on the track, took off her helmet and cried, "I can't. Not tonight, you guys. Not tonight. I can't take one more hit. I can't get knocked down one more time." And everyone who was there reached in and helped her get up, because when we're on the same team, that's what we do, we help each other get back up.

After practice we went to our usual dive bar to have a few beers and a few shots and we shared stories and laughs about the ups and downs of practice, and of life. Over all the sweat and the bruises and beers and the whiskey, the red ribbon of some of the most incredible friendships was wrapped all around and through each and every one of us.

One of the women from my team, *my person*, made it a point to talk to me every single morning until my divorce was final. I came to expect and look forward to her call. Some days I complained about everything. Some days I cried because of all the emotion and stress. Some days I laughed, thankful that there was nothing new to share. She was the one person who knew the entire story, start to finish, because she made it a point to listen to me every day. Because of her daily call, there was at least one person in this world that I wouldn't have to relive every painful detail with when asked, "How are things going in your divorce?" She probably saved me mentally more times than she realized. During that time the darkness was so strong and I was fighting so hard to find some light. One of the things she told me was that even though there were so many clouds, the sunshine would start poking through, and eventually the sun would overcome the clouds and I would have bright and shiny days again. I believed her because I had nothing else to believe in. I'm glad I believed her; it took time, but I learned she was right.

Lots of the skaters cross-trained and played other sports. One asked if I'd ever done a triathlon. I hadn't. She suggested I sign up, so I did. I trained for the run. I had a mountain bike and started riding that more. I didn't train for the swim because I used to be a lifeguard and figured I could do it. Stupid move. I'll never forget standing in front of the lake I was supposed to swim across on the morning of the race and thinking, *What in the actual hell did I get myself into?* I think I nearly died during the swim that morning, and my transition times were a little slow, but after all was said and done, I was thrilled that I had actually finished the race. Not only did the women in derby inspire me to do a few triathlons, but they also inspired me to run a half marathon and commit to a pretty consistent yoga practice. I loved it. I loved skating. I loved the sisterhood. But it was a lot of time committed to the athleticism of the sport as well as volunteering for the league. Even though I was going through my divorce, those were some of the best years of my life.

I was an active Shevil for five seasons until, ultimately, injuries sidelined me from the sport. Retiring due to injury is no surprise to anyone who has skated. Over those years I had multiple broken bones, a pretty wicked concussion, and two ruptured discs. Roller derby coach Bonnie D. Stroir is credited with saying, "Most seem to find roller derby in transitional periods. We ruin our bodies to save our souls, and for some reason that makes perfect sense." I could relate. My heart and my soul were pushed to the absolute limit, so I made my body do the same. Some people claim that derby causes divorces. For those of us who've been there, I'm pretty sure we'd all agree it's the opposite. It's like what Bonnie said: Many of us find derby when our relationships have failed and we're in a transitional period. Those of us who aren't receiving the support we need to feel whole somehow find each other in derby. And within those friendships, we find the courage to live our lives how we need to live them in order to be our truest selves.

Over the years I watched some husbands and wives grow closer because of the sport, learning to be there for each other differently, allowing for their partners to go after their dreams. Those husbands and boyfriends and lovers (derby widows) became fierce supporters of their partners and the teams and the league, and while they probably put up with some crazy league shit that no one else will understand, they became better partners and friends because of it. Those couples, the ones that learned to love each other with a freedom so fierce that you couldn't help but feel their passion, those are the ones whose partnerships have survived life's other jolts and interruptions. It's beautiful when people support each other with a love that's so fiercely free.

I met some of the most incredible, powerful, brilliant women and men as part of the league, and those are years that I will treasure forever. Those years moved me from divorce to living single, from fear to freedom. During those years I made some of the most beautiful friendships in my life. And because of those friendships, I found more love and authentic living than I ever possibly could have. It was the beginning of figuring out how to love myself more deeply. It was the start of my coming home.

Derby may have broken my body, but it definitely saved my soul.

JOLTED

➤——————→

We all know you need the rain in order to find the rainbow, but sometimes the jolts and interruptions of life come so fast and furious it's hard to believe the storm will ever end. Those storms don't always leave a person feeling very semi-charmed or sun-kissed, that's for sure. When people ask about my divorce or about certain stories in my life, they say, "You actually went through that?" And while I have experienced my share of awesomeness and I make it a point to live my best life no matter what curveballs are thrown at me, there has been some stuff that seems pretty unbelievable. That context is important here. Choosing to face these blank pages and share stories to connect and heal was prompted by two major jolts in my life—my career and health—which were inextricably intertwined.

The reflections, the travel, the healing, and the culmination of this book would not have happened had my life not been completely and utterly jolted.

I've already shared a bit about being laid off, which, in my freedom mindset, I chose to view as a blessing. Truthfully, prior to my layoff, I'd been walking on professional eggshells for months if not years. I was constantly wondering if members of my team or I were going to be hit with the job loss that comes with the excitement of a company's "transformation." On the advice of an HR coach, I had taken a position in a newer area of the company. I was told this would be a great opportunity to learn a new skill set under some great leaders.

Unfortunately, I landed in a role with a boss who *clearly* did not like me, and, quite frankly, I wasn't exactly fond of her, either. I felt excluded from conversations I should have been a part of, and she never offered me a "seat at the table." I dealt with her as much as I needed to, knowing she was only a temporary fixture in my career. As it turned out, I was the temporary fixture.

In the fall before my layoff, I spent some time on self-care, visiting one of my dearest friends in the UK. On the flight back, my lower back became so stiff it was difficult for me to straighten up and walk. I already knew I had two ruptured discs (thank you, roller derby), and the acute pain I was experiencing was familiar. After a week or so of the pain growing increasingly worse—high-deductible plans will make you put off an office visit with an orthopedic specialist—I called my doctor and went through the process of getting the initial visit scheduled, the order for the images, the MRI, and then, finally, the follow-up visit.

The thing about chronic pain is, if you have it, you learn to deal with it in one way or another. For me that was daily stretching, medi-tation, and medication. For the last several years I had been managing through all these mechanisms, but this flare-up was different. When I finally went in for the MRI, the doctor began by saying the discs looked significantly worse, and then recommended yet another round of physical therapy and injections, and as a last resort we could look at surgery. I'm quite certain I had no color left in my face. My pain and disappointment in the situation had absolutely done my head in, and I was on the verge of tears. His mouth was moving and I could hear no sound, all I felt was the fire of a pain that would not stop.

When he stopped talking, I took a deep breath in and exhaled slowly. In the moment of silence I made a decision. I wasn't going to live in pain any longer. I looked my doctor in the eyes and with a calm and steady voice I said, "Fucking fix me." He cocked his head to the side, surprised by my comment I'm sure. I went on. "I've been dealing with this pain for years. The flare-ups are getting worse and more frequent. I can't take it anymore. Please. Just fix me."

He started to talk about risks. I didn't even care. The pain was so intense I would have had surgery that day if he'd had an opening. I walked out of his office with prescriptions to manage the pain and inflammation, and a surgery date of March 22. That meant I would have to rest and medicate and wait for another four months. March couldn't come soon enough. I was finally going to get some real relief.

After my spinal fusion was scheduled, an interesting shift occurred. Once my mind resolved that my situation was bad enough to warrant having this surgery, it told my body that it was done fighting to hide my symptoms. As a result, there was a significant shift in my overall pain tolerance. What was once routine, daily pain was suddenly absolutely unbearable. My brain had let down the veil it had been holding up to mask the pain so I could pretend I was fine. I was no longer fine. Unless I was heavily medicated, I could barely sit at my desk. It was excruciating to stand up straight, and it was difficult to walk. When I got home from work every day I went to my room to rest, and sometimes I stayed there for the entire evening. I was a disaster. On my good days, I went through the motions of life with a halfhearted smile. On my bad days I stayed medicated and lying down as much as possible. My kids asked me how my back was almost every single day. I'd always smile and say, "It's a little sore but I'm all right," because that's what we moms typically do, we mask the pain and make sure everyone else is fine. I filed my disability and FMLA paperwork with our Human Resources department. I was approved for the time off work to recover and heal from the surgery.

About a week before I left the office for my spinal fusion surgery, my manager indicated that, had I not been approved for disability leave, my position likely would have been eliminated. Further, I should be prepared because when I came back after the 10–12 weeks of leave, the overall situation probably wouldn't have changed. My very authentic internal dialogue went something like, *So … what you're saying is … good luck on your surgery we don't really like you all that much so don't let the door hit you on the way out.* My self-preserving corporate-speak came out more like, "Thank you for making me aware of the circumstances. Is there an opportunity for additional head count by midyear?" The response indicated that even if additional positions were available, perhaps my skill set was not what the team needed at this time. I guess when you don't have a seat at the table, you end up on the menu.

After that meeting I immediately called a mentor, a vice president who worked in a different department. I explained the situation and she said to me, "Go get your surgery done while your benefits are intact. The right thing will happen and everything will fall into place." She had always given sound advice, and there was no reason to doubt her. Her message was exactly what I needed to hear. Despite my relative panic, I inhaled a breath of gratitude and tried to exhale the pain.

Within the next few days I saw a posting in a different department for a role that was perfect for me. I contacted the VP, an incredible leader with whom I had worked on previous projects. I formally let her know of my interest and qualifications. The people on her team were folks I had worked with before, and I reached out to them as well. I received a few notes saying how great it would be to collaborate again and that the team was pulling for me to get the job. It felt good to be recognized for the value I could bring to a role and a team. I felt confident that this was the next best right thing. When I e-mailed the VP, I was transparent about my pending surgery and recovery time, which I believed was the right thing to do. The response I received was as follows:

> *Thanks for your e-mail—great to hear from you. Unfortunately we have too much work so we would be unable to wait for your return from surgery to make a hiring decision. Wish you all the best!*

It was such a polite, concise message, but I couldn't help but think, would that have been the message if I had indicated I was pregnant? In this age of awareness around gender pay gaps and diversity and inclusion, this is how women are treated inside Fortune 500 companies. *You have great experience and you're a great fit, but we have too*

much to do, so your pending FMLA claim renders you incompetent
for a role change and ineligible for a transfer.

Then what's the point of FMLA? I was frustrated. I was in pain.
It felt discriminatory. Maybe it wasn't. Regardless, I didn't have the
energy or wherewithal to address it.

I called a girlfriend that night and explained the situation. After
she patiently listened to me pretend I was brave about surgery and
finances and my career and life in general, and after I got to the point
of feeling heard, we agreed that this was all just a bump in the road
and "This too shall pass." It felt good to just talk it out. This was part
of the journey. My life in between now and my return to work would
sort itself out, and, like my mentor had said, the right thing would
happen. My girlfriend and I started discussing my pending surgery,
which, thankfully, was just a few days away. She asked who was going
with me to the hospital. I explained that I was going to Uber there
and back so I didn't have to bother anyone. I made a joke that since
I'd be asleep I didn't really need anyone there anyways. She paused,
then asked how long I would be there. I told her I believed it was a
three-night stay. I ended my explanation by telling her that it really
wasn't a big deal.

There was an awkwardly audible pause. Then she shouted at me
through the phone, "Not a big deal?!" I immediately realized I was
wrong, and this surgery was, actually, a big deal. "You need someone
there with you. If you don't get someone, I'm canceling my family trip
plans and I'll be there. What if something happens? What if you need
someone to make a decision?" She went on for a bit and it finally sunk
in. "You really need to lean on someone for this." She was partially
encouraging but more so demanding. It was what I needed to hear.
I'm used to doing things alone, but this was one situation where I
really needed to rely on someone and ask for help.

I really hate asking for help.

I was raised to believe I was strong and independent. I was also
raised with the understanding that it was important to have a strong
network of family and friends. And somehow I felt that despite my

network I should not need to ask for help. I felt like I should handle things alone. I had somehow convinced myself that I didn't deserve help, and I would be a burden if I asked for help. Here I was, having a major surgery and on the verge of losing my livelihood, and I thought it somehow inappropriate to even bother to ask for a ride to the hospital. After this realization, I broke down and asked my parents if they would take me to my surgery. My mom agreed to rearrange a bit of her schedule so that she and my dad could be there. They also agreed to stay at my house with me directly following my hospital stay. I appreciated their help since I was starting to understand the magnitude of a two-level spinal fusion. I had been too busy surviving to recognize I needed assistance. Again ... gratitude.

On the morning of my surgery I felt fine. I told the nurse who was checking me in that maybe I should just postpone it. She smiled and said, "Oh hun, everyone says that." Maybe it was the adrenaline, or maybe it was the drugs, but I don't remember much past getting into the hospital gown. Actually, I don't remember much about the three to four weeks following the surgery. I know I was in the hospital for four nights instead of three. I know they had me walking with a walker. I know I told my parents to leave the room when I was doing physical therapy. I know my parents stayed with me after the surgery, but I only remember my mom bringing me toast. Once.

Quite frankly, surgery was a major jolt. It threw my normally independent self into a situation where I required assistance on many levels. It was the right decision to have the surgery, but it changed my life rather abruptly. This interruption demanded serious life changes.

After surgery, not only were there routine things that I could not do (temporarily), but I was also exhausted all the time. It was a massive daily accomplishment to simply take a shower. For about a month, a shower was my measure of daily success. Physical therapy started at five weeks post-surgery, and it was about that time I began weaning off the prescribed narcotics. The medication fog slowly dissipated.

My physical therapist told me over and over again, "Your body has one chance to heal right the first time. Slow down. Be patient and forgiving. Let it heal. Keep breathing."

Yet again, this was what I needed to hear. I was accustomed to pushing my body to its limit, conditioning and cross-training to prep for the beating of roller derby. Now I needed to force my body to relearn some of the simple movements I had casually taken for granted just a few months prior. Perhaps more importantly, I needed to mentally learn to pause and give myself the time to heal. On the days when I was so exhausted I couldn't take a shower, I forgave myself and lay back down. On the days I couldn't stay upright long enough to make healthy food, I made frozen pizza. I relied on my kids to do housework and help me put on my socks. I tried to not feel like a horrible parent for missing some of their events.

I gave myself space and grace to breathe and heal. I religiously completed my PT exercises at home to the best of my ability. I began to celebrate my body for its ability to recover and heal from this major trauma, this jolt. I learned to accept that I was changed but still the same. And I began to shed the unrealistic expectations I held for myself given my new, bionic back. I learned to define my new life on the journey in between surgery and healing.

There is power in slowing down and moving out of survival and into recovery, and then into living again. Recovery forced stillness. It made me spend time in my own thoughts, reassessing my mindset and analyzing whether I was standing in fear or in freedom, and I often fluctuated between both. Over time I learned to offer myself forgiveness for not being able to accomplish all the daily tasks that I wanted to accomplish. I began to pay attention to other important things, things for which I'll be eternally thankful.

Here are some gratitude journal entries that helped me stay in a positive space while I relearned the abilities of my body.

I have gratitude for . . .

Watching my daughter do her homework on my bed in my room. She is so beautiful and confident and grown up. Listening to her and her friends tell me stories about their days and their adventures is priceless.

Having long conversations with my son and his friends ... They are more thoughtful than I believed them to be ... Also thankful for him helping me put on my socks.

Watching college and NBA basketball playoffs with my youngest son since we both have a love for the game. He is so tall and mature and intense about the sport and has a wealth of player stats and facts in his recall that blows my mind.

Cuddling my dog while she patiently stays at my side. She is so sweet and so loyal and I am so her person.

Consciously releasing the worry about my work e-mails and my work calendar. [Thank Goddess I did because, ultimately, they certainly very consciously released me!]

Having dinners and lunches and playing cribbage with friends who visited without expectation for me to entertain.

For watching spring melt into early summer right outside my bedroom window.

For walking in the neighborhood with my girlfriend who tolerated my slow pace and inability to do great distances. She shared with me stories from her family and her divorce that were similar to mine—things that maybe we could have helped each other through had we started sharing much earlier.

As a mom who never had the opportunity to be a stay-at-home mom when her babies were infants and toddlers, having time to be with my kids became more and more precious with each passing day. One thing became crystal clear as I redefined my life: It is impossible to dream when you are in survival mode. Scrambling for a paycheck and running from a high-stress job to the chaos of home to parent drop-off/pickup for sports practice to the grocery store and on and on causes sheer exhaustion. The *busy-ness* of life with its onslaught of demands is all-consuming. It's almost as if this surgery jolted me into the life of intention and gratitude that I was supposed to be living, instead of the high-pressure, fast-paced, rat race life I'd grown accustomed to over the years. I was jolted into slowing down and breathing in these moments with my babies who are no longer babies but young adults. Taking the time to physically heal was the biggest commitment to self-care I had ever allowed for myself. As it turned out, it was the time I needed to emotionally heal, as well. Slowing down was exactly what I needed to reset my vision and reclaim my worth and chart my course for the rest of this beautiful life.

DIVORCE

➤——→

Life is so messy. It's heartache and headaches and bedhead and tears. Then life is glorious and then it's messy all over again. It's hard to look at social media and believe that other people experience the same types of jolts and interruptions that cause us to have to redefine our own lives. In this day where we sometimes measure our value by number of likes and comments, we have to remember that no one's Facebook highlight reel is real. Every single friend on our friends list endures the craziness of life, and pretty much every one of them is using filters on their photos to enhance their looks. What we all need to keep in mind is that our unique life interruptions give us specific perspectives that are real and valid. The jolts that shape us prepare us for whatever life is about to hand to us. We are all attempting to live our best lives in between the peaks and valleys of our real life journeys.

When we only show the highlight reel and keep our behind-the-scenes stories secret, we bury the authenticity of our experiences, and sometimes squelch the light of our souls. Perhaps, like me, you've experienced fears related to potential job loss or a major physical illness or injury. Maybe you've been in survival mode, so burned out that you feel you don't deserve to take time for yourself, ask for help, or even take a break. It's no surprise that when you're trying to survive life as a parent, especially a parent on your own, it can feel like it's you against the world.

When it became public knowledge that my husband and I were getting a divorce, I experienced every emotion you can imagine. Mostly, I was afraid. I was in constant fight or flight mode, a completely natural response during any stressful situation, neither of which is a good option when you're trying to remain calm and be a good mom. I had a few relatives call me to offer encouragement and support, and a few who offered to drop everything and pray with me. While a great strategy for some people, this was not what I needed at the time. If my family reads this, some may say that regardless of my opinion, prayer is exactly what I needed, but I can tell you that what I really needed was help figuring out how all this was actually going to work. And a Valium. Maybe two.

I'm watching several friends going through divorces right now, some are hearing rumors of affairs, receiving inappropriate sexual advances, experiencing financial devastation, battling addictions, watching their kids systematically move between two homes, trying to navigate multiple competing schedules with one adult driver in the household, etc. Some of my friends are having to answer questions about their "failed marriages" from people who are so bold as to ask, and some are having to answer unasked questions from people who are so cowardly as to only discuss these things behind their backs.

As my friends experience their divorces real-time, I can't help but relive portions of mine. Unfortunately, in my situation, it feels as if the divorce never ends. Sometimes I feel as if I don't really belong in my community. Sometimes I struggle to balance my mom life with my professional life with my social life and my personal life. Sometimes I feel like every single-parenting decision I make is the wrong one and I'm hopelessly failing as a mom. While I'm trying to juggle everything, the bottom line is that I hope I'm doing right by my kids. To parent is to make a ton of mistakes and to live with guilt, permanently. Yes, to parent is to live with joy, but ask any mother and she will tell you there is a sense of guilt that takes up residence in the depths of your soul that makes you constantly question whether you're doing things right.

The truth is, "adulting" is hard. Adulting and raising kids at the same time is even harder. Adulting and raising kids with all the emotional distress that goes with co-parenting can be a shitshow. All of the complexities of adulting can kick up the darkness and make a person question her worthiness: *Am I worthy of being a mother? A wife? A partner? Was I ever a good wife? A good mom? Will I ever be loved again?* That fear mindset is a terribly painful space.

I'll never forget when the gavel came down at my divorce and everything was final. The last thing the judge said was something like, "I hereby grant the return to your maiden name." I was immediately both relieved and devastated. I was me again. But I was also not the me I used to be. The sound of finality in the gavel made me panic. I wondered if I did the right thing. I thought it was the right thing. Maybe it wasn't the right thing. I hoped it was the right thing.

Over time, the stress of life's unrelenting pace took a considerable toll on me. Work demands spilled over into evening hours, parenting demands were a round-the-clock endeavor, and my mind was fixated on the what-ifs of life. I was worried about failure. I was exhausted, and I was sad. I felt like, when I found something to be happy about, I couldn't hold on to it. I felt like I was drowning and there was no one there to help me. I finally called an over-the-phone therapist for an initial consultation. We discussed my thoughts and worries. I asked him if I was going crazy. He reassured me that I was not, but he also highly recommended that I talk to someone more regularly, to learn how to better manage my thoughts and my exhaustion. I realized I had allowed my internal dialogue to become an echo chamber of negativity and unworthiness, and I needed someone to help me climb out of that despair.

I wish I had talked to someone to learn valid coping mechanisms sooner. I wish I had been able to figure out how to breathe more deeply shortly after my divorce. It takes time to rise out of survival mode, and I needed support to do just that, yet I was afraid that if I asked for help I would be burdening others or seen as weak. I didn't want to tarnish any friendships or perceptions. All I wanted was to be semi-charmed and sun-kissed. All I was, was tired. Broken. Sad. Confused. And afraid.

Over several counseling sessions I developed new thought patterns to cope with the pain that came along with restructuring my family. Instead of reacting to every dark thought that entered my mind, I tried to actively practice the self-care advice from my therapist:

> *Pause. Rest. Reset. Give yourself grace. Forgive yourself.*
> *Forgive your partner. Stop questioning every move. Rees-*
> *tablish your boundaries. Repeat.*

Taking these words to heart and committing to them as actions were important steps on my long walk out of the darkness. The decision to slow down and navigate my emotions took conscious effort; it was critical to find my way through the messiness. That was (and is) the work of healing.

A girlfriend of mine just finalized her divorce, and she is in the process of resetting boundaries for herself and for others. It's amazing how bold people are with their assumptions and advances. For anyone on the receiving end of an unsolicited (a-hem) picture, you know exactly the boldness I'm describing. As we compared notes about the audacity of some of the interactions we have both experienced, we decided that one of the best phrases to use, whether out loud or simply in your mind behind a knowing smile, is, "I don't receive that from you." We can only control ourselves, so sometimes it's imperative to build a force field that keeps out the rubbish.

> *I don't receive that from you.*

She and I also spoke at length about this transitional period of figuring out life in between marriage and divorce and what friends and family sometimes say or don't say to you while you're going through the divorce process. Wouldn't it be nice if we could have a checklist to share with others about what to say or do when you're restructuring your family? I know I wish I had had one to hand out to my family members as an icebreaker or conversation starter when things got awkward, especially because I wasn't comfortable with the "thoughts and prayers" strategy. I liked the idea so much that I started a list of phrases and the internal dialogue that often happens:

Do not tell me I should spend time alone. (I'm worthy of companionship.)

Do not tell me I should date somebody. (I hate men right now, but if I tell you I'm on Match.com, *don't* tell me it's too soon! Maybe I need a distraction or a friend who won't judge about my divorce.)

Do not set me up with anybody. (Clearly, I'm not ready for a new relationship and how am I ever supposed to trust anyone?)

Do not tell me I need to eat more. (WTF am I too thin now?)

Do not tell me I need to eat less. (Are you saying I'll never get a man unless I'm thin?)

Do not expect me to be fine every single day. (I am not fine!)

Do not expect me to be depressed every single day. (I am still allowed to have happiness and I'm going to take it where I find it! Please don't make me feel like I shouldn't be happy.)

Do expect that some days I may burst into tears for no apparent reason; the triggers will come and the triggers will go. (Look. There's a family together and I'll never have that again!)

Do know that I need time to mourn and go through the stages of grief, including anger that may come up for no apparent reason. (Divorced? Oh yeah I'm fine no big deal I'm getting over it. OMG there's a family together I hate how people can just be together how can they stand being together all the time! I hate everyone. Now excuse me while I go cry because I saw a family together and mine is clearly not together.)

Do include me in your plans. (Even if I can't make it, an invitation makes me feel valued and worthy and loved.)

Do realize that I have been in survival mode and I have no idea what will happen next. (I have no idea what's in the cabinet for dinner and whether I have enough money to make rent this month so *please* don't ask me what I'm doing the first Tuesday of next month, Karen!)

If you ask me about what the future holds, try to understand that I am fighting for my life and my kids and my stability and my mental, emotional, and financial health, and it is virtually impossible to put forward any ideas of what the future could or should look like. Actually, just *don't* ask me about it. If you do, don't expect an answer, and if I feel brave enough to share something with you, don't you dare judge me. (Please just hug me and tell me it will be okay.)

Basically, if you have a friend who is going through a divorce, show up with wine, dark chocolate, and ice cream (or yogurt and granola, whatever your person prefers). Watch a crazy movie. Maybe a comedy. Be there with patience and authenticity and without expectation or judgment. Sit in silence. Or talk and laugh or cry. Just be. And bear in mind that, truthfully, time (and the help of a great therapist) will heal all wounds, but there still might be scars.

As I alluded to earlier, word-wounds are some of the hardest wounds to heal. They can echo in your mind over and over again and reinforce a fear mindset. Every time they are replayed, the word-wounds cut deeper than before. Even if the cut is small, it still hurts, and over time, it is like death by a million paper cuts. *You're selfish.* (Cut.) *No one will love you.* (Cut.) *You're damaged.* (Cut.) *All you will ever be is a part-time mom.* (Cut.)

All those thoughts need to be consistently and confidently counteracted with opposing statements so say this out loud: "I am beautiful inside and out, and I'm worthy of love. I am growing into the person I was intended to be. I am resilient. I deserve good things. I am a caring and nurturing human being and I am doing the best that I can and that is enough. I am enough."

Now go back and read it again. Say it out loud three times to reprogram your brain and clear out any of the negative self-talk.

Some of the stories we tell ourselves need to be fact-checked and balanced with a friend or a therapist. As my girlfriends and I got real with each other about our personal fears relating to our divorces, we realized we had some of the same questions and some of the same ideas. On more than one occasion my friends and I have discussed the following:

What if I am never loved again? I'm so confused. Was I ever even properly loved in the first place?

If I get a boob job, am I being too vain?

What does a mommy makeover entail and how expensive is it really?

Will anyone love me if I don't look like I used to?

Why am I equating love with how I look?

God, I hate waxing—well, no one is going to be down there anyways so should I bother with the expense?

Where the hell did these wrinkles come from? Should I get Botox? Am I being selfish if I get Botox?

Am I going to die alone? What if I'm alone forever? What if I fall and I really can't get up and my kids find me dead and naked on the floor in my bathroom because I slipped coming out of the shower?

Am I not lovable? Why do some of my friends who have gone through divorce seem to be bouncing right back into relationships? What's wrong with me that I don't have that?

What if his family makes my kids hate me? What if I've done something to make my kids hate me? Ugh. *I* hate me.

Was everything my fault? I feel like everything was my fault. It all must have been my fault.

If anyone offers to pray for me one more time, I'm going to lose my shit! Just stop praying and send me money. And Tito's. Because I don't know how I'm going to survive this mess.

These are all real and valid thoughts. Once my girlfriends and I started getting raw and transparent about what we were really feeling and thinking, we realized how normal we actually were. Surprise, we weren't crazy after all! We were just trying to figure out who we were now that we were no longer married, and also no longer who we used to be. It actually made us more human once we began to share our vulnerabilities in love instead of hiding our thoughts in shame. Changing relationships, aging, vanity, wondering about love and raising kids, and questioning everything are all very real. Sometimes we need to talk about our journeys through the seasons of life. We need the wisdom and perspective of those who have experienced or are experiencing the same things.

None of us is alone in dealing with the internal and external pressures of society, image, and perception. Whether you're single, dating, married, widowed, divorcing, or any shade between any of those categories, these pressures are very real. When we have genuine conversations and ask the questions in our hearts, we allow for the darkness and light to wrestle with each other in a fairer fight. We all must continue to ask ourselves what we really want and more importantly what we need to learn from all the emotions that come with all of life's changes.

And for Goddess's sake, if you've thought it through and you really want the boobs, you don't need anyone else's approval or permission. Just go ahead and get them.

ACUTE STRESS DISORDER

»———→

S omewhere along the way, I decided that in order to love myself, I needed to make peace with my own story. I couldn't hate or wish away any of the bad stuff, I had to face it. I needed to walk into the fire to have it cleanse me so I could begin again. I also decided that I wanted, no I *needed*, someone to help me navigate the heat of those flames. I needed a therapist.

Our overall mental health impacts the choices we make and the lives we live. In Western culture, we often associate shame with the vulnerability it takes to open up about our emotions and seek therapy. In some recent conversations with friends who have backgrounds in psychology and coaching, we speculated about the sum of what humans are at our core. We are everything we've experienced in life, multiplied by traits passed down in our DNA, our wiring, and our thought patterns. We discussed how our chemical and energetic makeup not only creates us but also pushes us to make certain decisions. We even talked about how our learned behaviors can guide us to choose our partners in life, often the wrong ones. We concluded that if we don't learn our life's lessons when they first are given to us, we're going to keep going through difficulties to teach us that unlearned lesson, over and over again.

There has historically been a stigma around seeking help for mental health, yet it's difficult to truly learn from our experiences without talking through them. Speaking with an unbiased third party can help with that. One of my girlfriends who appears to not only be very personally fulfilled but also have a very happy marriage told me that she's been seeing her therapist monthly for *years*. I was surprised at first, but what she said next made perfect sense. She explained that if she only talked to her counselor when things were bad, she wouldn't be able to deeply trust and lean on her when there were life jolts and interruptions. While I had never actively thought of counseling as inherently bad, that sentiment moved me to celebrate the idea of therapy.

I met my current therapist about three years ago. I had originally seen one that I didn't particularly like or trust, so that relationship didn't last very long. I saw another one that was kind and thoughtful and who, after about four visits, promptly retired. It wasn't until maybe a year after that, when I was going through some heavy stuff, I was referred to a new therapist. I called to set up a meeting, half thankful to have someone to talk to, and half mortified to have to go through this introductory process all over again.

As I walked into the new therapist's office building I noticed how old it seemed. Dark. Dirty. There was a large, soothing waterfall inside the entryway and a modern metal artwork sculpture that appeared to be faces looking in multiple directions above the reflection pool. *Nice touch for a psych office*, I thought to myself as I pressed the "up" button on the elevator. I closed my eyes and listened to the water while I waited for the elevator. The sound of the water made me feel calm. When I opened my eyes and stepped into the elevator, I noticed how dimly lit the building seemed. I arrived at floor three and walked to my new therapist's office door. It still felt dim and dirty. I got called back to her office. It was even more dim, but much less dirty, which made me feel a little better. I wished I could still hear the waterfall.

We started our conversation with pleasantries, and my therapist asked me what brought me to her office that day. I smiled at the familiarity of the question. I explained what I had been experiencing as of late, and as she took notes she sometimes made eye contact with me and sometimes seemed to intently make eye contact with her paper. At moments her eyes widened, and I wondered if she thought

I was actually crazy. Was I? I didn't know. I only knew I was trying to survive and maybe be successful, even though I didn't know what success actually looked like anymore. She nodded a lot. She kept writing while I kept talking. When she asked me questions, I found her voice to be quite soothing, kind of like the waterfall. I wished she was the one doing most of the talking.

Toward the end of our first session, she said to me, "I'm diagnosing you with acute stress disorder." Now it was my turn to widen my eyes and nod. I figured those words made perfect sense given everything I had just thrown at her, but I also expected that it was a made-up diagnostic term for insurance coding purposes. We set up a second appointment and I carried on about my day, rushing back to work and then rushing home and then rushing to whatever events were scheduled for the evening.

What led me to schedule that first appointment was a whole ton of crazy that had happened all at once. I was in the middle of a home sale/purchase. I had started dating someone who seemed interested in an actual partnership, but who turned out not to be what he seemed. My house that was for sale was robbed while my kids and I were enjoying a family vacation at Disney World. I didn't want to lose a pending sale because of the robbery so I moved up the closing date, leaving us with no place to live. I unexpectedly had to put my dog down, and that beautiful brown creature had been my best friend, my ride or die. On the painfully silent drive home from watching her fall asleep for the very last time, I blew a tire. You cannot make this shit up.

Even when remarkably difficult situations get thrown at you all at once, time has a way of marching fearlessly on, regardless of whether you're ready for the next day, or even the next moment. I admit, I coped with all that had happened by staying tolerably drunk for about three months. Another glass of wine? Yes. Actually, please just pass the bottle.

After the robbery, I put what was left of my stuff in storage. The kids spent more time at their dad's house. I stayed at the house of the guy I was seeing. He kept my wineglass full and made sure I ate food every once in a while. I wanted to be numb. I closed on the old house and paid off my student loans. I closed on my new house and moved what was left of my stuff from storage into what was supposed to be our new, safe home. I called ADT to set up a home alarm system. And some lovely new friends who learned of my situation gifted me a brand-new puppy.

I tried to keep a happy face for the kids but it was mostly me just going through the motions. My boyfriend was getting more and more possessive, but it was masked as protection. It felt off, but I was too much in shock to recognize or do anything about it. Survival mode. Then I got an anonymous message that my so-called boyfriend was a super-player on the "casual encounters" ads on Craigslist, followed by screenshots of actual messages and pictures that all but proved that this man was not really who he had claimed to be. When I worked up the courage to approach him, he denied every accusation, made it clear that someone was setting him up, and implied I was the problem for believing lies about him. Classic gaslighting.

All of these things added up to a breaking point. A work colleague had picked up on my deterioration and asked if I was all right. I wasn't. She was the one who referred me to my new therapist. I'm thankful she recognized my pain and suggested I schedule an appointment. I was so overwhelmed and confused that I could not take one more day of anything. At the end of one of those first sessions, my therapist suggested that maybe it was time for some significant self-care. I decided to go camping somewhere up north in the woods. Alone.

It was the best thing I could have done. Removing myself from existence in survival mode forced a kick-start of some serious reflection and baby steps toward recovery. For a few days, I was basically off the grid and alone with just my thoughts to keep me company. I read. I journaled. I cried. I hiked. I sat in the sun. I sat by the fire. I breathed in the fresh air. I only spoke if and when I felt the need. I unpacked all the thoughts in my brain into a journal, and I sobbed my way through the majority of the words. Upon returning home I promptly put that journal away, wondering if I would ever read it again. Sometimes it just makes sense to let your fears flow out of your soul and onto the paper and then simply put them away forever.

However, I recently overheard someone say, "Silence is the sickness, and conversation is the cure." Those words confirmed for me that sharing was the right thing to do, no matter how scary and no matter the consequence, because perhaps someone else can relate to those feelings and might be empowered to have a curing conversation as well.

SELF-CARE JOURNALING FROM THE WOODS

➤——→

CONTENT WARNING: *These next chapters include modified excerpts from my actual journal from the woods. They are included here in a spirit of truth and authenticity, and as an emotional context in the journey of living in survival mode and with Acute Stress Disorder. The words included here may be triggers for some, so please only read if you are in the emotional state to do so.*

On the first morning of my self-care camping trip I woke up in the fresh air feeling completely alone. I had expected to start the morning fresh and clear, but all I felt was murky. Heavy. Emotionally confused. Maybe I expected that part of my journey to be easier. Maybe I was naive.

I'd spent the last several months watching my fifteen-year-old daughter experience her first heartbreak after true love, and it destroyed me in ways I never expected. Also, my dog died. She had been my best friend for eight years, and I had to choose the day she took her final breath. My house was robbed. It was totally cleaned out—a professional hit job—while I was with my kids enjoying the happiest place on earth. My corporate job pivoted in responsibility and expectation for what felt like the hundredth time, having changed more times in the last twelve months than in the last twelve years. I settled some post-divorce litigation (court, *again!*) with my ex-husband. I moved. I watched one son finish his select baseball season and my other son finish his select basketball season.

It all had been too much.

Sometimes people compliment me by saying things like, "You're so strong!" And seriously, if I hear one more person say those words to me I'm going to lose it. Being strong means I shouldn't have to ask for help, that I'm always fine, so when I do ask for help, I feel like I'm taking advantage, since I'm supposed to be strong. "Fine" and "strong" are curses that breed mediocrity ... and exhaustion.

After discussing all life's recent interruptions and my absolute exhaustion with my therapist, I decided I needed a break from everything. And everyone. So I drove across the state of Wisconsin to Minnesota to visit my girlfriend from college. It was just what the doctor ordered ... that perfect sense of comfort without pressure, a few glasses of wine, some appetizers. And so. Many. Laughs. Fate brought us together 20 years ago. Love will ensure we are never apart.

After my visit with my girlfriend, I drove to northern Wisconsin, hoping to find a walk-up campsite at a state park. Unfortunately, the last available sites were taken moments before I arrived. I decided to hop back on the freeway, enjoy the scenery, and stop at the next campsite for which there was a sign. I ended up at a lovely mom-and-pop owned campground (52 years and going strong!) that seemed tucked out of the way enough for me to enjoy some peace and quiet. When I arrived, the ground was damp and covered in fallen leaves and browning pine needles. The owner was riding a golf cart. He was round and weathered and had slightly crossed eyes. When he welcomed me I reassured him I was well over twenty-one, and he directed me to "the office." The office was the sun porch of a home that had clearly acquired everything it could possibly need over the last 52 years. The paperwork was handwritten, and I provided cash payment. The round man with the crossed eyes took the two bundles of wood I purchased into his golf cart and escorted me to my site.

My assigned campsite was private. I was on the very end, about three sites down from my nearest neighbor. You could fit a half dozen tents on my space alone, so my lone three-man looked incredibly small. My space was in between everything. To the west there was a steep hill, and at the top was a landing with more sites; to the east was a wooded slope that led down to a lake. It was beautiful. It was peaceful. It was all by itself. It was exactly what I needed.

I set up my tent on my own. I'd never done that before. It was a little tricky but eventually I worked it out. Actually, setting up camp on my own was easier than trying to coordinate and take care of anyone else, adult or child. I sat at the campfire and drank my one bottle of beer. Eventually, the flames grew tired.

I did too.

There's something about sleeping in the fresh air that's both exhilarating and exhausting. As I closed my eyes and drifted off into that space between asleep and awake, I wondered why everyone who knew I was camping by myself told me to be careful. "You're going by yourself? Really?" they'd ask in disbelief. "Yes. I've been alone for a while now. I'm pretty sure I can handle it."

I'm strong, I thought, *I can handle anything.*

I laughed at the irony. Being strong is what got me to this point of exhaustion. I knew I needed to unpack that.

Sleep eventually came but it wasn't easy or restful, since I knew the purpose of my time in the woods was to do the work. I needed to process and understand everything that had happened in the last few months. I needed to walk through the firestorm to let the flames cleanse me so I could start again. I needed to reset my boundaries and my goals. I needed to wrestle my dark and find my light.

I wasn't feeling strong anymore. I felt like everthing was spinning and I was just reacting. I was making decisions out of fear and circumstance, not from strategy and conviction. I needed a hard reset.

I recently listened to *Carry On, Warrior,* by Glennon Doyle, and I heard her tell me to write what is on my heart, because people need to hear real stories. So I decided to do just that. As I wrote my own memories and stories, I began to recognize that I'd been coded to perform and coded to achieve. There were so many awards and accomplishments that I was proud of, and then this subset of things that just felt like *busy-ness* and survival. Especially during recent years there was so much happening that I always needed something to take the edge off the constant pressure to go/do/be/perform/deliver/prepare/ celebrate ... all of it. I wondered if I'd ever really learned to pause and just breathe. I didn't think I'd ever been out of survival mode long enough to enjoy that privilege. I wondered why pausing and breathing feels like a privilege. Breathing in the good shit and exhaling the bullshit is something we all should have the opportunity to do.

I became aware at an early age that all humans have unique journeys. Once I became acutely aware of the experience of living, I decided that I wanted to have every human experience I possibly could. I devoured books to understand other people, other places, other worlds. I signed up for every sport I could play. I took music lessons. I adopted a pen pal from Japan to learn about Japanese culture. Overall, I was a good kid.

I attended a Lutheran parochial school for K–8, then another for grades 9–12. We had excellent teachers who had a passion for education. There were eleven kids in my eighth grade class, so we all knew each other quite well. There were three or four girls in my grade during any given school year. We understood the expectations for staying within the Lutheran lines. Through my younger years, there was one girl in my grade who took it upon herself every day to make it either a good day or a bad day for me. I went to school every morning wondering if she would be my friend that day. She and a few others took dance classes at the dance studio in town. I did not. I played sports. I was tall and muscular and thick. She and her friends were long and lean and elegant. I wanted to be like them, but I wanted to be me, too. One time one of the girls had a party across two of our grades, where all of the girls in both classes were invited. Except me. I was hurt but I tried not to let it show. It solidified my suspicion that I didn't exactly fit in with the girls. So I started to hang out with the boys. I often played football or softball at recess instead of sitting on the playground talking with the girls. It was easier that way. It also felt more productive. Who wanted to just sit around and talk during recess?

One year a family transferred into our school/church. They were rumored to be financially struggling, so the entire congregation rallied around them. The oldest daughter was three years ahead of me. She was teased daily for picking her nose and eating it. It made me sad that people picked on her. We were Christians. I thought we were supposed to raise people up despite our differences because we're all children of God. In addition to being teased for this habit, she also wore clothes that were mismatched and ragged. She wasn't always showered, and her thick glasses made her an easy target for additional bullying. One day on the playground I'd had enough. I fought back on her behalf. I found the courage and fire inside to cast a verbal spell of justified anger back on her tormentors. I'll never forget her look of shock, relief, and a glimmer of hope and friendship when our eyes met. I'm not sure if anything changed for her after that incident, but I knew I had done right by her. I also became acutely aware that everyone who was made to feel "less than" needed an advocate. I learned that part of my purpose was to give my strength to others when they needed it.

We had daily religion classes, and starting around third or fourth grade there were things that didn't sit well with me. It seemed there was hypocrisy in some of the teachings; the words and actions and explanations didn't always line up. We often had open, more challenging dialogues in our fifth through eighth grade years, but it always came back to us memorizing what the teachers and pastors told us to memorize, backed by the three to five Bible passages supporting the assertions taught to us by the ones who determined our final grades.

Grade school was a relatively safe place, where we all seemed to play by the same rules. Outside the school walls it was a slightly different story.

At the age of fourteen, I had my first kiss. We were in the back of a school bus, at night, on the way back from a youth trip to a water park. This boy had been paying special attention to me all afternoon. He made me feel like I was different, not just "one of the guys" who played sports at recess. I don't really remember it being gentle and special as our lips met. I just remember his mouth splitting mine open and his tongue darting in my mouth. I remember panicking ... wondering if the other kids were watching and if I should really be doing this. Then his hands were up my shirt ... grabbing and pawing at me. Suddenly the zipper on my pants was yanked down. All the while his face was pressed against mine and his tongue was in my mouth so I could say nothing. I crossed my legs. Hard. He was crossing a line. I wish I'd understood the whole thing was disgusting. I didn't. I thought it was how things like this must happen. We got back to the bus stop/parent pick-up area, and all the kids filed off the bus. We went home.

I never heard from that boy again.

In high school I dated some boys and made out a few times, and one boy in particular I was sure I was going to marry. This was a Lutheran high school, after all, and the ultimate adult goal was to serve the Lord and get married and have children of God who would also be fishers of men. At the age of about fifteen, I started hearing rumors about me, rumors that I was a slut. I really wasn't sure why. I didn't even fully understand what that meant. One time on the way out of study hall, we were all pushed together, and a boy from the class ahead of me pressed up against my back. I felt his breath on my neck, and then his hand from behind, in between my legs. "You know you want it," he said.

I froze. I didn't want it.

In that moment, what I did want, was to disappear. I said nothing. After he let go, we walked into the hallway. He laughed loudly with his friends. I walked silently in shock. I decided to pretend it never happened.

Later that year I was walking out of art class and a boy two grades ahead of me cornered me in the stairwell, where he crudely detailed what he would one day do to me sexually. He told me what he knew he would make me enjoy. Again, I froze. I said nothing. He walked away like it never happened.

I never told anyone.

That summer when I was hanging out at a friend's home, the dad repeatedly grabbed and smacked my ass and told me how hot I was. It made me freeze like I did in the stairwell. Everyone laughed it off, including his wife. Because they all laughed, I convinced myself it was excusable. Only now as I look back I realize it wasn't.

These experiences shaped my thoughts and expectations on sexuality and the role of women in relationships, and they confused me. Despite these brazen advances, and being called a slut and on occasion a whore, I didn't have a boyfriend and I'd never had sex. I thought about all of it a lot, but I didn't understand. My internal dialogue was in a downward spiral. I was too afraid to discuss any of what had happened because I didn't want to get in trouble, and I didn't want to get anyone else in trouble, either. I kept it all to myself. My self-esteem suffered. Maybe those times where I had been grabbed and cornered were my fault.

During my sophomore year in high school, I decided to own some of this. I'm not sure if I felt empowered to make some choices on my own, or if I felt cornered by the rumors I was constantly hearing about myself. I decided to lose my virginity. I found someone willing to help. One night we went to his house, snuck up to his bedroom and got undressed. He put on a condom. He crawled on top of me. He asked if I was okay and if it felt good. It didn't feel good at all. It just felt like he was sweaty on top of me and he was all red and ruddy and it kind of hurt. "Yes, it feels good," I lied. A few minutes later he finished, got off me, and stood up, clearly proud of himself. I looked down and saw blood between my legs and also the condom, which had evidently fallen off. I panicked. I thought something was really wrong with me because of the bleeding, and since the condom fell off, I might be pregnant.

He said, "Don't worry," and his words somehow reassured me. Then he said, "I'll do the laundry," and I realized his only concern was his sheets. I said okay and thank you—as if I owed him some gratitude.

I stared at the condom in disbelief. As an afterthought, he told me not to worry because there was no way I could possibly be pregnant.

I got dressed and left his house. I drove home. I went to bed under my covers, safe in a home with parents who loved me, and I cried. I was cold. I was shaking. I was in shock over what had just happened. Over what I did. Over how it happened. I hid my bloodstained underwear in the back corner of my second drawer in the tall dresser. When I knew no one was watching, I took it outside and burned it.

Now if they called me a slut, I guessed it was true. Because I had sex. One time. I would be strong about it, because that's what I was. Strong.

Around that time I was introduced to pot by a friend, a fellow Lutheran in my grade but from a different high school. I had always wanted to try it. This was all part of the fully human experience — I wanted and needed to understand this phenomenon. I had actually learned how to inhale Newport Lights cigarettes with the sole intent of being able to someday inhale a joint. Some of my friends who tried it got headaches and hated it. When I smoked, I found it soothing. It kind of made me care less and care more at the same time. It felt good. It was a release I didn't know I needed. I began to find out who smoked and who didn't, and I thoroughly enjoy the company of those who did. Through this newfound network, I developed new friendships. These new friends didn't call me a slut. These people didn't judge. They had unique points of view and different styles. They were artists, readers, music lovers, storytellers. What I noticed most about this crew was their undying loyalty for one another. They kept one another's secrets and had each other's backs. They accepted me, and they had my back, too.

I hung out with these new friends until the end of high school. And even though I smoked a lot of pot, I graduated third in my high school class. Many of my new friends weren't going away to college, but I knew I wanted to eventually leave. For my first two years I went to a community college to save money. Even there, I had the ultimate freedom explosion. The class schedule was amazing, the content was shared through a non-religious lens, the debate was inspired, and the people were absolutely fascinating. It was the first time in my school life that I didn't have a Lutheran pastor–led religion class. It was the first time in my life that I had a philosophy class led by an atheist professor who didn't judge anyone's Christian beliefs, but rather encouraged a viewpoint on life from a different perspective. It was the first time I studied biology without the caveat that evolution is based on lies and God created the world in seven days, no matter what anyone else says. In between classes, my friends and I frequented a local coffee shop where the philosophy professor would stop by and debate and discuss whatever was on our minds. I felt like the whole world had suddenly opened up.

In my second year of community college I met an older man who had just returned home from the military and was in some of my classes. He was intriguing. Charming. Charismatic. People tried to warn me about him, but I didn't believe them. I dated him. My parents hated him. I stopped going home at night so I could be with him. He made me feel like I was the only one who mattered. It was fun and it was free. Until I found out I wasn't the only one he was so fun and free with. I had a mental breakdown. I felt ashamed and embarrassed. When we finally talked (yelled) about it, he pushed me down, headbutted me, and told me I was a slut.

There it was again. I was a slut. I shut down. I apologized. I realized the whole situation was my fault. (WTF was I thinking … obviously it was not my fault.)

Over the course of the next several months I came to realize that this man was not right for me. I had blended the ideas of sex and love, and I had lost my sense of self-worth somewhere along the way. It was clear he was only using me. I had even considered marrying this man. What was I doing? I was angry at him. I was angry at myself. I ended it.

After our breakup, it took a little time, but we remained friends. One day he asked me to go with him to get an apartment. I agreed. I was moving away to a new university in the fall, so I was trying to be nice. We went up to his new one-bedroom space and he shut the door. I was ready to leave, to say our final goodbyes. He had other ideas. I told him no. He wouldn't listen. "One last time." He was too big and too strong. I just lay there until he was done.

I was a slut.

That fall I moved across the state to finish my bachelor's degree at a four-year university. I got lost in a bigger crowd and found myself with a small group of friends. We drank booze and laughed a lot. I was happy. I kept good grades. One night at the dorm, the man who had raped me showed up. I didn't know exactly how he found me, but I didn't want to cause a scene in my new life with my new friends, so I placated him and spent time with him. He spent the night. I sent him away in the morning. He wanted to try "us" again. I did not. On the way home, he got pulled over and fined for driving without a license. He called me to tell me it was my fault and I was a slut. I literally laughed out loud. Perhaps being in new surroundings on my own terms provided clarity, because this time, I let the word simply fall off of me. It had been used against me, without cause, one too many times.

Around that time I visited my sister who lived in Ohio. I wanted to escape the chaos of life and her home was the perfect retreat. I lay on her couch and she painted my toes. I was jealous because she was always smiling and patient. I think she was jealous because I was always trying to stand up for myself and act brave.

As she brushed OPI "I'm Really Not a Waitress" red on my toes, she commented, "God built you strong for a reason."

"I know," I responded. "I know." She smiled at me with her big-sister smile. I smiled at her with my little-sister strength.

Why the fuck did God curse me with strength?

I graduated from college with honors and moved to Milwaukee for graduate school. Graduate school was hard. I had to show up and read and actually try. At Christmas that year, the boy I was dating proposed to me. I accepted. We set a date. We made arrangements. A few months later, he asked if we could "push out" the date because he wanted to live with the guys for a while. I accepted. After all, I didn't want to seem too needy. I called the hall, I called the pastor, I called the photographer to reschedule. No problem. A few months later, he wanted to push it out again.

This time, I refused.

I gave him the ring back and told him I didn't want to speak to him. Ever. I felt like he had tricked me into believing he loved me; he had tricked me into believing I was lovable. I was depressed. I failed, again, in the relationship space, but this time, in front of everyone. I had a wedding dress and bridesmaids and deposits on all the things that go along with having a wedding. It all came crashing down, and I was so embarrassed.

But you're strong, said the voice in my head.

Not anymore, I responded to the voice. I spent days in bed, and I used all my paid time off. Eventually I found help in group therapy and Prozac.

Within a year, one of my guy friends who had a two-bedroom apartment approached me about moving in with him. He said he wanted a roommate to share expenses. It made sense for me financially, so I did. He was a good friend. I didn't like to go out much at the time, and he started to bring me pills and booze and we ordered pizza and stayed in and watched a lot of TV. Then, one night, he tried to have sex with me. I was taken aback. I was not a slut and because of all our conversations I thought he knew this. I said no. I said that I thought we were friends and I didn't want to cross that line. He stared at me with hate and anger. He left the house. I figured he would just blow off steam and come back later. I went to my room to go to bed. When he came back to the apartment, he called me out to talk with him. He had a gun and some bullets. He told me I might as well kill him. If he couldn't have me, life wasn't worth living.

I was scared he might kill himself. I was scared he might kill me.

What in the actual fuck is happening here?

I didn't know what else to do so I hugged him. I tried to wrap him up in love and acceptance. I told him it would be okay. I had no idea if it would be okay. I hugged him for what seemed like hours. Eventually he fell asleep. I pushed through the haze and the disbelief of what had just happened, and made a fast plan; I moved out while he was at work the next day. I never saw him again.

Shortly thereafter, I met the man who would become my husband. We had a whirlwind romance and I got pregnant the first time we had sex. Or maybe it was the second. I took a pregnancy test and sat on the bathroom floor in his apartment. The two lines showed up immediately. *FUCK*. And all the emotions came at once. I left the bathroom and told him.

He said, "FUCK," and all his emotions came at once.

We eventually decided to make a go of things. I knew I was keeping the baby. It would be up to him if he wanted to stay. He chose to stay. We learned how to be partners and parents, together. Despite others' judgment masked as concern, we made it, for as long as we could. Our daughter was born in February of 2002. She was absolutely perfect.

She saved my life.

She gave me purpose.

She stopped me from being afraid.

She taught me true love.

He and I decided to get married about a year later. We got married largely for insurance purposes (how romantic) and also because it was largely considered the "right" thing to do.

My marriage to my kids' dad yielded a lifetime of learnings. And for each lesson learned I'm eternally grateful. Without him I wouldn't have my three beautiful babies, who are now young people rapidly approaching legal adulthood. He and I tried to be a family in the best way we knew how. In the end, for us, it just didn't work.

A host of reasons exist as to why our marriage didn't last, and, truthfully, all of it is painful. I could chronicle the devastation and how we both immaturely made decisions out of fear and the need to survive, but I'd rather write about the learnings. The challenge with the heartbreak of my divorce is that I carry it with me as failure, buried under a smile and good posture and, most of the time, silence. What I learned is that when you stay silent for too long, people expect you to simply be strong (semi-charmed and sun-kissed) so when you ask for help or work through the appropriate systems to ask for help, people don't always believe you need it. I also learned that not all people live life according to the same rule set, and because of that, creating a safe place for honest communication without judgment is critically important in maintaining relationships. I learned the importance of forgiveness, not only for others, but also for self. Living in a state of constant question and blame is mentally, physically, and spiritually exhausting.

Finally, and maybe most significantly, I learned to be thankful for all of life's good and happy moments as well as the bad ones, because all of the moments are opportunities for learning new thought patterns to better navigate a beautifully imperfect life.

COCO

➤——→

We rescued Coco when she was estimated to be five years old. My then-husband and I had taken the kids to the humane society for a "field trip." This beautiful brown dog was so sweet and docile. My son, who was actually five at the time, saw her and said, "Mama, this dog wants us." I tried to shush and dismiss him, but one look in her big brown eyes and I knew it was true, she wanted us.

We took her camping with us that first weekend and she crawled into my sleeping bag and slept curled up by my feet. She was definitely our family dog, but she was immediately mine. Over the next three years we all bonded and she seemed to make our lives complete. When I showered she waited for me by the closed bathroom door, and she waited at the top of the stairs of our second-floor condo for me to get home from work every day. She was always there to greet me, bright eyes and wagging tail. Coco and I had an unbreakable bond. Somehow, even though she wasn't mine from a puppy, we belonged to each other.

She came with me full time after the divorce, which was both awesome and overwhelming. I often traveled for work, and I knew I'd need help. Also, how was I going to handle vet bills and food and who would walk her?

We sorted out our schedule and eventually fell into a pattern. We discovered our new normal on this journey in between being married and whatever was next. Coco loved all of us through the divorce as only a dog can. She stayed by my side on the couch and in my bed. On the days I didn't have the kids and felt so dark and overwhelmed that I couldn't get out of bed, she gently nudged me until I would take her outside. She became my running partner as I set my sights on completing a half marathon. As she aged, her brown fur turned silver, and she spent more and more time lounging and sleeping in the sun. She stopped running with me after about two summers of training, and I noticed she moved more slowly while trying to get up the stairs.

As she aged, Coco became more human and less dog. Sometimes she sat with me at the dinner table and I fed her steak off a fork. She always ate the crusts off my pizza. She warmed my feet under the covers, and we spent endless date nights on the couch together snuggling and watching movies. She listened to me when I told her about my day. She let me hold on to her and cry. She never judged me or made me feel less than. She accepted me exactly as I was.

Coco was my best friend.

She taught me loyalty.

She gave me all the love I didn't know I so desperately needed, and she expected nothing in return.

When Coco started having accidents in the house, I thought it was a sign of her age … and maybe I was leaving her alone too long. I consciously adjusted my work hours to make sure she had less time without going out. At the beginning of May, I took her to the vet and we treated her for a urinary tract infection. Coco was put on a ten-day regimen of antibiotics. She perked up after a day or two, and I dropped her off at our friends' home to puppysit for us while I took the kids on vacation.

My kids and I spent the next seven days at Disney World for my daughter's all-star cheerleading competition, and also for our own sanity and family bonding. It was a week of fun and sunshine and pool time and adventures. For most of our vacation, our spirits roamed free. Disney accommodated my daughter's food allergy. The kids were all old enough to be semi-independent at the parks. As a mom, I was able to watch my kids relax and just be kids and have fun. It was magical.

On the ride home from the airport after our vacation, the kids were trying to get out of going to school the next day. They kept pushing and negotiating and we all kept laughing. We pulled up to the house. It was dark on our street, about ten thirty p.m. I noticed that the outside garage lights weren't on. I figured the puppysitter must have turned off the lights when he dropped off Coco.

I opened the garage door to pull my car inside, and for some reason, the space seemed remarkably empty. I made a flip comment about us leaving the lawn mower in the backyard. We grabbed our bags and filed toward the door. When I opened the front door I immediately noticed a cord from the pancake griddle on the floor and that the throw rugs weren't in the right places. Coco came walking up to me with her head down, as if she'd done something wrong. I paused for one second to hug her and love her when several things happened at once:

I noticed the living room TV was gone.

My laptop was not in its usual place on the counter.

Nothing was on the counter.

My ten-year-old started screaming, "It's happening again!"

I turned around and saw that the washer and dryer were missing.

I began to run through the house, frantic, to be sure no one was there. Perhaps this wasn't the smartest move, but I was definitely more fight than flight in that moment. My daughter was sobbing. My youngest was in a panic. My thirteen-year-old asked if he could call his dad. In a fog, I told him yes. In my brain, I repeated, *I can't go through this again. I can't go through this again.*

Just two years prior, my home—in our beautiful, safe, suburban neighborhood—was robbed while I was traveling for work. I was on my way home from California when my daughter called, alerting me to the fact that the back patio door had been smashed in. She was levelheaded enough at age thirteen to call the police and stay with neighbors until the police and I could get there. That time, it was a smash and grab. Anything worth perceived value was taken. My jewelry and heirloom coin collection were gone. Supposedly the investigation ended with the suspects in jail—a junkie couple. The wife died of an overdose, and the husband was in prison on other multiple theft charges.

That was awful, but this was devastating. The police were baffled by not only the amount of things taken, but also the types of items. The thieves had taken valuables, not-so-valuables, items large and small. They also had taken personal items, like my shampoo and conditioner, both new and used. Food was taken, including the entire contents of my spice rack and all of my canned items and nonperishables, except the canned artichokes. My freezer, stocked with homemade soups, was empty.

Some of the furniture was left. Most of the clothing still hung in the closets. Most major appliances were gone. The lawn mower, the kayak, and the camping stove were all gone. The few jewelry pieces my daughter and I had that were worth anything, including our memories, were gone. My late grandmother's fur coat—the only thing I had that still faintly held her scent—was gone.

The most devastating thing that the thieves took was my family's safety. My family's safety was gone.

Hearing my ten-year-old screaming, "It's happening again! It's happening again!" while my fifteen-year-old daughter was yelling, "It's gone! My jewelry from Grandma is gone!" while my thirteen-year-old tried to be strong and said, "Mom, I'm calling Dad," was a cacophony of madness that will forever echo in the corners of my mind.

More than $22,000 in items stolen, and ultimately, insurance paid out approximately $13,500, due to policy limits, replacement value, and applied deductible, of course.

To complicate matters, I was moving. We were closing on that house on June 12 and moving to our new house on June 19. It was May

18. The proceeds were going to finally pay off my student loans. This new house was a little bit bigger and had a fenced-in yard for the kids and Coco. I was devastated at the thought of losing the house sale.

Given that the entire situation was a complete cluster, my "boyfriend" of three weeks let Coco and me move in with him temporarily until everything could get sorted out. I sold much of what remained at my house and put the rest into short-term storage. I tried to move forward and make sense of the violation. We pushed up the closing date. The buyers were appreciative. I was relieved. I would still be able to pay off my student loans and use the remaining funds for my small down payment on our new house with the fenced-in backyard.

We settled into our temporary living arrangements in this in between time. It was awkward, but it was all right. We tried to maintain some sense of normalcy in our patterns and routines. The kids stayed at their dad's a little more often, and I tried to be productive at work and live out of a suitcase as a guest in my boyfriend's home. Thankfully, I was working on some analytical projects at the time, so travel wasn't a requirement and I could work "from home" until my situation got sorted.

Coco, however, didn't seem to be adjusting very well. She continued to have accidents, even though she had already completed her antibiotic prescription. She wasn't eating much, which is normal when there's a major interruption in circumstances, but she even shunned scrambled eggs, the breakfast she and I had shared many times over the years. My beautiful brown dog with the silver face and the wise brown eyes never turned down scrambled eggs. I knew something was wrong. I took her back to the vet. Tests revealed that, at estimated age thirteen, my best friend was showing signs of kidney failure as well as gallbladder and liver deterioration.

Coco was dying.

I could spend a few thousand dollars trying to medicate her. She would need to be hospitalized. There was no guarantee of her recovery. My vet helped me weigh the options. There was no right answer. I decided that on Wednesday morning, Coco would gently go to sleep for the last time.

On Coco's last night on earth, she ate two McDonald's cheeseburgers for dinner. She went on a long walk with me, and then a shorter walk with the three kids. We took pictures with her. We buried our faces in her fur and breathed her in. We told her stories about how much joy she brought to all of us. She was loved. She was happy.

The next morning we drove to the vet in silence. We were called back to the room and Coco lay down on the floor ... calm, knowing, sad. That morning, she was down from her normal weight by almost eight pounds, which was quite a bit on a medium-sized dog. Her skin sagged. Her brown eyes looked tired. It was like she knew it was okay to go.

We took her outside and she sat on a blanket in the sunshine while the four of us petted her and told her how much we loved her. Her short fur was so soft and so warm in the sun. Eventually our vet came out and administered the drug that helped Coco peacefully go to sleep for the last time. We all had our hands on her as she sat ... then coughed ... then lay down ... and closed her eyes. All four of us kept saying, "We love you we love you we love you so much," so she would know it was okay to go. I remember saying to the kids, "Just keep saying you love her so she can hear your voice," and then, "Oh my *God*," while our vet put his hand over mine and told me it would be okay. Coco died slowly ... and then all at once. And then she was gone. We sat with her outside on the blanket until it seemed unhealthy to stay. We all said goodbye and pet her soft fur and touched her sweet face for the final time.

Coco died on a summer morning in June, one month after our home was robbed, and two weeks before we moved into our new home. She never got to play in our new backyard or run up the stairs to wake up the kids. I can't wait to see her again, healthy and playful, waiting for me at the rainbow bridge.

Two days after Coco died, the kids sent me some pictures on our group text. They were playing with these adorable puppies—miniature long-haired dachshunds. They were just a few houses down in the neighborhood. When I walked up to them and saw the little bundles of puppy joy, I started sobbing uncontrollably ... full-on ugly crying. I was struggling tremendously with Coco's passing, and these brand new puppies flooded me with memory and emotion. They were six weeks old, cuddly and absolutely adorable. We all took turns passing them around and loving on them. The breeders were socializing the puppies from early on so they were happy to have neighbors walking by stop to chat and hold the pups. All were spoken for except one: Hazel. Hazel had been spoken for, but that person had called two days earlier to let them know he had decided to go with a more local breeder, so she was now available.

"Mom, can we get her?" was the question. The answer was an immediate no. I couldn't step into puppy ownership, especially with a purebred price tag. I told the breeders the story of Coco, and we cried together. We talked about what a gift dogs are for us and how they teach loyalty and unconditional love. I offered to advertise their newly available puppy or foster if needed. We helped them pack up the pups and said goodbye, exchanging numbers just in case something came up.

As we began the short walk back to the house, my new friend began calling out to me, "Candy, Candy!"

I turned around and asked if I had left something behind. I checked to make sure all three kids were accounted for. I said a quick silent prayer that none of them had done anything stupid.

She said, "We believe every great dog has a great story, and Hazel was being released back to us at the same time you had to put your Coco down, so we want you to be her story. My husband and I want to bless you with her."

The tears were immediate. The gift of this puppy was infinitely generous. I hugged her and cried. I couldn't believe it. Not only had this woman I just met given me this incredible gift but she did it in front of my children, showing them what generosity and abundance really look like.

Charlotte Hazel Lauren Kitty Winston Lilly Roo is now known as "Charlie Girl" and is the coolest sidekick ever. She doesn't replace my best friend, Coco—no dog ever will—but she eases the pain left in my heart from her death. And Coco would have loved her.

The first night of my solo camping trip was Charlie's first night in a tent. When we got settled in she crawled inside the sleeping bag and slept by my feet, just like Coco did.

REENTRY

$\longrightarrow$

Sometimes I feel like I don't belong in my own life. Like my body feels a bit foreign (this could be age), my house doesn't feel like a home (it does take awhile to get settled), and I just don't fit in (have I ever really fit in anywhere?). Most of my closest friends are scattered across the US and the world, actually, and I feel more temporarily at home with any of them than I feel a sense of belonging in my own home and community.

As far as life milestones, I've been incredibly fortunate. When I turn around and look back at the highlight reel of my life, sometimes I'm impressed with important accomplishments and achievements along the way. After all, I've always believed you can do whatever you set your mind to. However, when I dig past the highlights, I'm sometimes overtaken with sadness. Despite my achievements, I sometimes still feel like a failure. My marriage failed. My engagement failed. I didn't stay a virgin until I was married (holy Jesus massive evangelical biblical fail). I've disappointed the people around me. I've tried to date and failed. Miserably. I keep hoping for happy endings and believing in fairy tales. I've always believed in the good in people only to be deceived. Failure all around.

My parents have loved me through the ups and downs of life with patience and grace. They've shown up to help me when I needed help, just like they have for all my siblings. I know it breaks their hearts to watch me endure life as it has unfolded, so I try to stay steadfast. I try to stay strong, because sometimes it's easier to smile and nod than it is to explain the emotional devastation of all the jolts. I guess I've tried to shield my family from as much of my heartache as possible to avoid them being any more disappointed in me than they already are. I wonder if my siblings ever feel like I do. I wonder if other people ever feel like strangers in their own lives.

It's a challenge when your belief systems don't necessarily line up one-to-one with your family's beliefs, especially when they had intended for you to come out of Christian school believing the exact same things they do, and to demonstrate it in the same ways. It's stifling when you're encouraged to spread your wings, to travel and study and expand your worldview, and you come back wanting to legitimately discuss alternate viewpoints, but suddenly you're perceived as an elitist for defecting from the status quo. It's really hard to swallow watching the unwavering defense of "conservative" political stances based on religious beliefs when it seems that the party line is held on principles that fly directly in the face of the teachings of Jesus.

It's even harder when the people who are closest to you or who want to be closest to you prefer to not discuss important topics at all. The silence is deafening.

It has become clear to me that when the conversation with someone ends, the relationship is usually over. I also believe that when we choose to cut off certain topics of conversation, we begin to squelch out what might be meaningful pieces of the relationship. Sometimes it's part of a tradeoff: *I want to maintain a cordial relationship with my uncle, so I choose not to engage in political topics with him.* But sometimes, that avoidance marks the end of a relationship: *My partner refuses to talk with me about his political views and values. He keeps pushing me out. How can we grow in trust if we can't have those difficult conversations?* When the topics are important, silence is not an option. Consciously choosing silence is to consciously disengage or disconnect. It isn't always bad, but it can be a slippery slope. After all, you can't say the wrong thing to the right person.

A girlfriend once told me that she believes we're all on the river of life, and it takes work to get down the river, lots of time and paddling to make good progress. When life gives you lessons, you must face them and learn them, or you'll get stuck on the river. You will likely need to learn the lesson over and over again until you accept the learnings, make changes, and move on. Holding these lessons in silence keeps us stuck. Isolated. Unlearning. Un-healing. Strangers in our own lives, stuck in between the being and the knowing, never moving any further down the river.

I've met people who seem to be receiving the same shit lessons over and over again. And I, too, have found myself in those seemingly unbreakable patterns. I sometimes watch my kids in the same cycle. The first instinct is to look outward: "It's the teacher's fault!" "I can't believe he said that to me." "She's got a lot of nerve to treat me like that." Going into the woods alone forced me to reflect on and try to more consciously understand the role I play in my own patterns, to do the messy work of healing, to move out of survival mode. Paddling down the river of life allows me to spend more time in the grace of knowing. So now, in times of struggle, rather than looking outward, I try to silence my mind, open my hands with palms to the sky, and ask with an open heart, "What will you have me learn?"

My story is filled with amazing moments and milestones and riddled with pain hidden under masks of "strength" and being "fine." The truth is, I'm not fine anymore, and I'm done being that cursed version of strong. I'm embracing my vulnerability and authentically sharing my truth in the hope that maybe it will help one other person share her truth, and then another, until we have an army of truth tellers ready to stand in love and hope instead of fear and exhaustion. I'm a better mom and a better human when I'm standing in love and hope.

I need to do better at only allowing people and things around me that offer love and hope. If they make me question my worth, and if they don't bring me peace and joy, I need to remove them from my life. Permanently. I might be different and have different ideas, I might have issues that I need to overcome, but I am beautifully created to live my own authentic life. I need people around me who will encourage me to stand in my own power, not encourage me to trade my self-worth to live a life of expectation and mediocrity. I need to remind myself that I am leaving the woods and my time in self-care, and reentering a world where sometimes even the people closest to me won't understand my boundaries, but I need to set them in order to protect myself, to heal, and to keep paddling down the river of life. I refuse to apologize for or negotiate my own authenticity.

When I came out of the woods I immediately broke up with that man who had helped me after the break-in, but who claimed he wasn't on Craigslist casual encounters. Despite his kindness, I couldn't look beyond the behavior (and evidence). It wasn't fair to him or to me to stay in a relationship where the trust was broken.

When I came out of the woods I called my mom to tell her I had not been eaten by a bear, since that had been one of her primary concerns. She was happy to hear my voice and I was happy to hear hers. After we hung up I made a mental note that healthy families are made up of healthy boundaries, and I needed to be okay with that.

When I came out of the woods, I drove five hours with my puppy on my lap and gratitude in my heart. I was proud of myself for walking into the darkness of the storm, facing the depth of my pain, and finding the sunshine on the other side.

When I came out of the storm, I looked up acute stress disorder. I laughed when I discovered it's a real thing and not just a bullshit diagnosis to make sure insurance companies cover the visit. Psychiatry.org defines Actue Stress Disorder as follows:

> *Acute stress disorder occurs in reaction to a traumatic event, just as PTSD does, and the symptoms are similar. However, the symptoms occur between three days and one month after the event. People with acute stress disorder may relive the trauma, have flashbacks or nightmares and may feel numb or detached from themselves. These symptoms cause major distress and cause problems in their daily lives. About half of people with acute stress disorder go on to have PTSD.*

I guess her diagnosis was not only a real thing, but also pretty damn accurate.

Now at least I can be open about why I startle so very badly (read: often collapse in fear) when someone sneaks up on me, even if they aren't trying to sneak. Now I can be honest about why sometimes I feel like a stranger in my own life. Now I can begin to further understand why I sometimes react to things the way I do and why it's important for me to consistently focus on healing. I can breathe deeply and accept my journey in between the good and the bad, and appreciate that all my life experiences have shaped me into the woman I am today.

I can now let go of being strong and pretending to be fine, and I can focus fully on healing and coming home to my own body and soul.

3

AUGUST ADVENTURES

"Travel not to escape life,
but so life doesn't escape you."

-UNKNOWN

FINDING YOUR TRIBE

➤⟶

A s I grow older in age and hopefully in wisdom, I spend more time reflecting on the concept of who is in my circle. I wonder who is truly part of my tribe. I can distinctly remember childhood experiences that felt uniquely positive because I was in the company of people with whom I connected both energetically and emotionally. I remember going to bars and concerts and sporting events with my best friends and thinking that the energy seemed to tangibly move when we walked into places together. Conversely, I remember the distinct nauseating feeling my intuition kicked up when I was in the wrong place or with the wrong people. It feels better to be with people who have the same character, values, approach to life. And, actually, life seems to shift for the better when you consciously choose to spend the majority of your time with the people who are in your tribe.

I've come to learn that tribes evolve over time. Some individuals flow in and out, and if you're lucky, some stay constant and ultimately share a long and storied history with you. My tribe has spanned across different friend groups and grown over various experiences and years and locations. One of the beautiful things about my tribe is that the people within it seem to show up, even when you least expect it, and when you least recognize how badly you need it.

Just before leaving on my self-actualization book trip, I went on a canoe trip down the Wisconsin River. Twenty-four of us were in the group, two to a canoe, and we planned to tent camp on a sandbar halfway through the two-day trek. This was the sixteenth annual trip for the organizer of this particular group, the husband of one of my fellow roller girls.

I was lucky enough to get invited to my first canoe outing with this group seven years ago. I committed to going, but in the days leading up to the trip I was arguably in the ugliest part of my divorce. I had been spending the days before the canoe trip at my parents' home, trying to reconnect with my roots, spending time with old friends, and eating my mom's home-cooked meals. Basically, I was sleeping in my childhood bed trying to imagine my life with a different endpoint. Or a different midpoint. I was trying to find my life in between this space of failed marriage and newfound freedom and scary single parenthood. It wasn't pretty. My entire situation was a hot mess and I was an emotional wreck. I convinced myself that everyone would have more fun on the canoe trip without me. I decided that I shouldn't go.

The morning of the canoe trip my phone buzzed at 6:00 a.m. I unlocked the screen to find messages from two of my friends from roller derby texting to make sure I was coming. I tried to gracefully decline the invite. I explained it was better for me to not bring everyone down with my sadness and negativity. I did not want to spend two days crying in front of my friends and the random others who were just looking to kick back and enjoy the river. But they didn't let me off so easily, and they insisted that I come along. I explained that I didn't have any food prepared for the two days, all I had was my clothes in my backpack. I didn't even have my tent or my cooler with me. They removed every objection. One friend said I could sleep in her tent, and the other friend said she would have food for me and take care of me.

Take care of me.

That in itself was enough to knock me off my own legs. At this point in my life, especially, I felt as if I had no one to take care of me. Hell, I was pretty sure I didn't even know how to take care of myself. Here I was, in the middle of my divorce, emotionally exhausted, yet I believed I was expected to be strong and handle things and navigate my life without asking for any help. I was in the middle of my darkness. I was actively wrestling it. I believed I was failing not only at my marriage, but also at my entire life.

After a bit more of their prodding, I decided to go. I wasn't sure if it was the right thing, but I didn't want to regret staying behind, and they seemed to genuinely want me to come along. I got in the car and drove ninety minutes to the designated meeting place. They welcomed me with open arms. We ate breakfast together at the diner and they reassured me that coming along was the right choice. My mood was lightened by having friends who wanted me around, even if they had to take care of me.

That weekend was a great experience. My friends talked and laughed with me and I was able to leave my worries on the river. They gave me a new perspective. They made me feel like I wasn't alone. I bonded with some of the rollergirls I hadn't spent much time with, and I met some new people I hadn't previously known. My friends let me sleep in their tent and they fed me. I felt taken care of in a way I really hadn't felt before. This was my tribe. I decided right then that I would go on the annual canoe trip as often as I possibly could.

Fast forward to seven years after my maiden voyage. I remained on the annual canoe trip e-mail list, but I had not been able to attend since that first year due to family commitments and kids' events. The year I undertook writing this book, despite having just gone through a spinal fusion surgery, I decided to attend. My physical therapist worked with me on exercises to prepare me for paddling. She told me as long as I got a good night's sleep on an air mattress I should be fine. The organizer of the trip assigned me to partner with one of his friends, a strong paddler who could handle the canoe on his own if the twenty-two-mile expedition got to be too much for me and my back. On the morning of the trip, I met my canoe buddy at the designated breakfast place and promptly thanked him for "taking one for the team" by being my partner. He assured me that everything would work out just fine. I couldn't help but feel immense gratitude that a complete stranger agreed to basically take care of me if I couldn't carry my own weight for the weekend. After breakfast, when we got to the place where we put in, he carried my cooler and the heavier items down the slope to the canoe. He did it without question or accusation.

He helped take care of me. He was immediately part of my tribe.

Paddling down the river is a beautiful, peaceful, amazing experience. Paddling down the river with two dozen friends who are equipped with water guns and booze is a beautiful, amazing, super-soaking experience, and it's ridiculously fun. We laughed during the water wars as the sun beat down on us in the perfect August Wisconsin weather. After several hours of paddling and a few food and drink breaks along the way, we set up tents to camp on a sandbar in time to watch the sun paint the sky in purples and blues as it set behind the trees. I brought along my unicorn onesie (no feet) because I thought it would be magical for camping—and it was. It was just comfortable and ridiculous enough to be absolutely perfect for the night. (Yes, I'm a forty-something woman and I have a unicorn onesie. Don't judge.)

The campfire was blazing. The beers (and White Claws) were flowing. The stories were rolling and we were laughing and happy, relaxing under the starlit sky. The river was peaceful and the moon was gorgeous. It was a perfect night, sitting amongst the good energy and friendly love of our tribe.

All of a sudden the temperature dropped. It happened so quickly it felt like walking into a refrigerated room at the grocery store, except in this case, the refrigerated room had somehow walked into us. Then, out of nowhere, the wind picked up. As if we were one body with one head, twenty-four humans collectively turned to look toward the wind, and we all saw a storm literally rolling toward us on the river. Within a millisecond, the stories and laughter stopped. Silence.

"This is not good," a voice said.

When the organizer of this trip, who has sixteen years of canoe and camping experience on this very river, says "This is not good," you know it is *not good*. In the moments after he said those words, everything seemed to turn upside down. The fire began to blaze horizontally with the wind, and the rain blew sideways off the river as well as down from the sky. All of us ran to our tents for shelter. I dove into mine, zipped up, and hunkered down to wait for the storm to pass. I sat alone in my tent, covered under the sleeping bag, safe and protected. My tent was over twenty years old. It's the same one that took me alone into the woods a few years ago. It's seen a ton of weather, and it has never, ever failed me. I had reception on my phone and plenty of battery, so I kept myself occupied by texting friends. I stopped mid-text when a gust of wind tore the rainfly off my tent and wrapped it around the side pole. The rain immediately assaulted my tent from all angles. I didn't know whether to laugh or cry. I waited for a few minutes hoping and praying that the storm would blow over. For a moment I believed that I could will it to stop. It didn't stop. As the rain kept coming down and the thunder clamored around me, it dawned on me that I actually might not be safe. The water was rising on the floor of my tent and I was absolutely soaked. I'm accustomed to doing things on my own, but this storm was wicked, and I was afraid. The friend I was texting messaged me:

> *Are you crazy? You're alone? Get into someone else's tent!*

That message pushed my fear over the edge. I ran out to the nearest tent with a light on, and I knocked on the flap. I didn't know whose tent it was, but a familiar voice answered, "Candy, get in here!" Within a split second the flap was unzipped and I was in the tent with one of my girlfriends and her boyfriend, sharing their queen air mattress and a blanket.

My tribe, taking care of me, again.

None of us got much sleep, and, thankfully, the storm eventually passed. At one point my friend asked me what time it was and I answered that it was 4:41 a.m. We decided to leave the relative safety of the tent and assess the damage. It was still pretty dark, but the river had come up significantly. As we walked around, we noticed that it had risen up far enough to fully engulf the bonfire we had sat around just hours earlier, and had it raised up any farther, it could have taken over our village of tents. What we also realized was that we only had five of our twelve canoes. We only panicked for a moment; we were relieved to find that more canoes were pulled up on the other side of the sandbar. We walked over to find four, for a total of nine canoes. We were missing three. That meant that six of us were literally up the creek with no paddles. And no canoes.

Overwhelmed and slightly defeated, we patiently waited for the sun to rise. I sat in my not-so-magical unicorn onesie in my soaked camping chair digging my toes in and out of the cold, damp sand. I was shivering. I was cold. I was exhausted. I was in pain. All my muscles were tense, and I had failed to do the one thing my physical therapist had told me to do, get a good night's sleep. As far as sitting, no position was comfortable. My trusty tent was now uninhabitable so I had nowhere to lie down. Completely frustrated, I wanted to do something productive, so I took an inventory of my camping gear. Although my tent was still standing, the rainfly was wrapped around the left side pole, and everything inside was soaked, including my pillow, my sleeping bag, my air mattress, and my backpack with all my clothes. When I lifted up my backpack a full tap stream of water drained from the bottom. My tent was ruined. My back was aching. And my canoe was one of the ones that the river had taken during the storm. I wanted to rest. It was five in the morning. I went back to my chair and turned it to the east to watch the sunrise, and also to hide my face from everyone in case the tears came. I decided this was the dumbest idea I ever had. I couldn't believe that I did this trip just four months after back surgery. I was upset that my awesome tent was ruined. I was cold and wet and frustrated. I cried.

Just then, one of the women with our crew came over to see if I was okay. She offered me some ibuprofen and brought me a bottle of water, which I very thankfully accepted. I think she sensed I needed to be alone so she didn't ask questions, but her quiet thoughtfulness and understanding made me feel a little bit warmer in the misty cool of the early morning.

The sun started to come up over the horizon. I watched it set the sky on fire, and I focused on being thankful for so many wonderful things in my life. As the sun climbed higher the air grew warmer, and I decided to change out of my unicorn suit and put on my swimming suit. Out of all the soaked clothing items I had with me in my backpack, it was the one thing meant to be worn wet.

I got dressed. It was still early and pretty chilly. When I got back to the group, one of the guys asked if I wanted his Army blanket to keep warm. I was so grateful that he offered. I wrapped up tight in the blanket. As my body temperature rose, my muscles relaxed and my shivering stopped.

As everyone began to ease into the morning, two girls I used to skate with offered me a dry tank top and pullover to keep warm. Again, I accepted. I was so very thankful that they offered.

A few minutes later, the woman whose tent I slept in had coffee percolating and cheesy hash browns and scrambled eggs cooking over a small fire. The smell of the food and coffee in the fresh morning air was delicious. Savoring hot breakfast in the great outdoors is one of the most satisfying experiences in the world. I retrieved the fresh strawberries and muffins I had packed in my cooler, some of the only things I had brought that were not completely soaked. Someone provided a bottle of mudslide to use as a creamer for the coffee. We all shared cups and plates and forks.

While we gathered and ate an incredible breakfast, we talked and laughed about the stormy events of the last seven hours. I learned that two of our tribe members had come to check on me during the storm, but I was already safe in another tent. The sun rose higher and the air grew warmer. We laughed about three of us sleeping on a queen-sized air mattress. We finished the food and cleaned up camp. The ibuprofen and caffeine kicked in. I was thankful to be with people who were willing to take care of me, who took care of each other. I imagined red ribbons running between all of us.

These are my people. This is my tribe.

It came time to figure out how we were going to get the six of us without canoes and all of our gear downriver to the take out point. After some debate, two couples decided to portage over to land and call for a pickup. My canoe buddy and I decided we would like to stay for the duration of the trip if we could work it out, and with that decision being made, our supplies were promptly divided between canoes, and seats were MacGyvered for us to ride on for the balance of the trip. At that point, some of my friends and I had a brilliant and unorthodox idea: we would blow up my air mattress so the two of them could tow it behind their canoe, and I could lie on it to stretch out my back and relax while being pulled down the river. Floating downriver on an air mattress? Yes, please! That was almost as ridiculous and magical as my unicorn onesie. We knew we had to try it.

Everyone laughed as we got ourselves situated. We tethered the mattress to the canoe with a bungee cord and assumed our positions. And guess what? It worked, and it was awesome. I felt no pain laying sprawled out on that air mattress on the water under the sun. I napped while they paddled. My physical therapist would have been happy. They handed me cold drinks and sunscreen when I needed it. It was absolutely perfect.

After about two hours of paddling, we found a canoe downriver stuck on a log on a sandbar — ours! My shoes and hoodie were still inside, as well as both paddles. It was a Christmas (in August!) miracle! Our tribe gathered around the runaway canoe, we got ourselves sorted and prepared to paddle. My canoe buddy offered to pull me on my air mattress if I'd prefer, and I probably should have taken him up on that, but instead we deflated the air mattress and paddled together. Those final hours on the river in the sun were perfect. We found the other canoes and towed them back with us. We stopped for lunch when the sun was at its highest point and we all talked and laughed about the storm. We replayed the discovery of the missing canoes. We discussed how lucky we were that the river didn't get so high as to flood our whole camp. We marveled at the fact that two of our guys had paddled downstream for an hour hoping to find the runaway canoes, only to come all the way back upstream. Empty-handed.

We laughed at the idea that they put in three hours of paddling even before half of camp was awake! We relaxed in the water under the August Wisconsin sun, and even though some of us had just met the day before, our bonds of friendship grew closer, our red ribbons binding us together.

The woman who brought me the ibuprofen described the canoe trip perfectly. "It is our confession, catharsis, and redemption."

She was exactly right.

When we made it to the end and took our canoes out, we hopped on the bus to get back to the cars. As we rode back, my heart was overflowing with happiness. I was (and am) so incredibly thankful for the entire crew of people who looked out for me and cared for me when they didn't have to, who made the stormy times adventurous and fun, who brought me the ibuprofen when I needed it, and who laughed with me after the crying. The entire weekend was semi-charmed, and after two full days on the river, we were all pretty sun-kissed.

My tribe is connected by our values and our experiences, and I am so incredibly thankful for them.

What I know to be true is that it's not just those people on the canoe trip who are my tribe. My tribe extends to the people who offer up the ibuprofen and the water and the coffee and food and clothes and shelter to *anyone* who needs it. My tribe includes the people who do that without asking who you are, where you're from, or whether you deserve it. My tribe does this in places locally, and at the borders of countries all over the world. My tribe does this after storms and hurricanes regardless of visa status or skin color. My tribe has compassion for all people and they make sure that the basic needs of others are taken care of. My tribe makes sure that we are bound by the red ribbons of respect and friendship and love. My tribe takes care of each other.

We'll take care of you.

AUGUST 11

→

Sometimes we just need a safe place to share our stories. When we find that place and then summon the courage to share our vulnerability, our light shines a little brighter, and we take one step closer to welcoming ourselves home.

On the day I wrote this, August 11, it was my dad's birthday. My dad, a hard-working, blue-collar Midwestern man, spent his years providing for his family. He was a construction worker, and even after he retired from iron work he spent many years working on farms and driving trucks to continue to not only provide for his family but also serve others. My parents provided a wonderful home life for me and my three siblings. Even when times were tight, we had food on the table and love in the home. My mom and dad are still together after fifty-plus years of marriage.

My dad taught his kids strong Midwestern life lessons over the years: *Show up early, work hard, stay late, outwork those around you, watch out for other drivers, watch for deer! Where there's one deer, there are usually more.* My mom and my dad raised us in the Lutheran church where we also memorized the lessons the teachers and church elders wanted us to learn about the Bible and the Christian God and Jesus. We attended church and worshipped as a family regularly. On Sunday mornings, we had donuts before church and brunch when we got home.

As my siblings and I reached adulthood and began to make our own life decisions, my dad watched us begin to live our lives as unique individuals. We made choices differently than he may have wanted. My parents held mini-interventions when we were veering too far off the path they had planned for us kids. At one point at about age nineteen I had been out all night with friends, only to come home and find the pastor of our church sitting in our living room. He, along with my mom and dad, wanted to discuss my current life choices and where I was headed. I'm pretty sure they thought I might be headed to hell. They wanted to invite me back to the church. I was appreciative but not very interested. I wanted acceptance, not guidance. If I wanted guidance, I wanted it in the form of coaching to define my life authentically, not to force conformity to someone else's ideals, even if those ideals belonged to Jesus Christ himself.

Learning to navigate family relationships, relationships we don't necessarily get to choose, while also learning how to choose ourselves, is tricky. I think about learning to set these boundaries with family like treading water when you can't touch the bottom of the pool. In the shallow end, you are safe. You are told what you can and can't do. You branch out to learn how far you can go and still survive. The deep end is where you are forced into self-reliance. You have to know if you're strong enough to swim to the surface or the side. My family liked to stay in the shallow waters where they could touch the bottom. We had fun playing and splashing there. It felt good and it felt safe. Once I found out I was a strong enough swimmer to explore the deep end, I began to tread water on the edge. Sometimes I stayed to splash around with my family, but other times I ventured into the deeper waters where I learned more about who I was in my soul ... who I was called to be.

Some of us are born to wade in the shallow waters of safety, and to stay where we know we can stand. Some of us are born to figure out if we can swim. Some of us love the water and are born to dive in and see how far we can swim on our own. Some of us need to spend time treading water where we can touch both the floor of the shallow end and taste the freedom of the deep end. Some of us are still trying to figure out if we should jump in.

When I was sixteen, I tested the water in all of the ways. I loved the safety of living within the framework of my Lutheran family's expectations, yet I was enamored with experiencing all the adventure in the mystery of life in the deep end. I was also in the throes of teenage angst, and I was wrestling with the darkness of having been called a slut. The safety of the shallow end didn't seem so safe anymore, and I was constantly told I was strong. I figured I was strong enough to swim.

Whether it was empowerment or rebellion or self-fulfilling prophecy, or some combination of all of those things, my internal dialogue prompted me to jump into the deep end and own this "slut" title by losing my virginity. When the opportunity arose, I thought I was taking advantage of the situation. I considered this young man to be my friend. He wasn't my boyfriend. Having sex with him was sort of like a trial run to see how things actually worked. Scientifically. While that maybe wasn't the wisest decision, the fact that the condom fell off at some point during the proceedings made things exponentially worse. I panicked, but he was cool. He was sure there was no pregnancy.

Easy for him to say.

I went home that night in shock. I was shaking. Panicked. Traumatized. What had I done? I just lost my virginity and it wasn't romantic or fun or even pleasurable, and it wasn't with my husband like Jesus wanted. It was just, well, technical, and it kind of hurt. And the condom fell off. This was a disaster. I could hardly sleep. I was bundled up under four blankets and quilts but I was still shaking and freezing. I just wanted to pretend it never happened. As I mentioned previously, I destroyed the evidence so all that was left of that night was my own private memory. Because there was no physical evidence, I could pretend it never really happened.

Then, of course, I was late. At first I didn't worry, my period was always a little off. But as the days turned into a full week, I began to get concerned.

I remember sitting through my sophomore classes thinking that not only was my life (as I had expected and planned it) completely over, but I had brought shame to myself, my family, my friends, and the church. I had literally failed the Lord Jesus Christ himself. I couldn't shake it. I stopped eating. I felt overwhelmingly sad. I withdrew. I was slow at basketball practice. My coaches noticed and told me to snap out of it. I called myself stupid in class one day (I was a 4.0 student) and the teacher reached down from his podium, smacked the desk in front of me with his flat palm, looked me dead in the eye and said with his booming, authoritative voice, "YOU. ARE. NOT. STUPID."

If he only knew how stupid I was. I jumped in the deep end, with a life jacket, but it had fallen off. I had sex. My life was over. I was stupid. And, it was now confirmed, I was a slut.

What's more, I was an athlete at a Christian school. As a sophomore I was playing junior varsity basketball and also suiting up for the varsity team. During warm-ups for one game my coach told me she didn't see me giving me the right leadership effort on the court. Leadership. Sure. How can I be a leader? I had sex before marriage. I was a sinner and a failure and I was going to carry that shame for myself and my family for the rest of my life. I played horribly in that game. I couldn't help but wonder if it would be my last time wearing our school's uniform. I was pretty sure the Lutheran elders wouldn't let teen moms suit up for varsity. I was convinced I didn't deserve to ever play basketball again.

The days went by and the shame and fear grew heavier and heavier, until one night I couldn't take it anymore. While I was drying the dishes in the kitchen with my mom after dinner, I started asking questions about being late and what that might mean. After a few minutes, my mom paused thoughtfully, and then her smile faded and the color drained from her face. "Is there a possibility that you might be ... pregnant?" After a dead silent pause that seemed to last an eternity, I stammered, "W-well … yes … I mean …" and immediately the tears started flowing—for both of us. Her tears were likely out of anger and fear and disappointment. My tears were out of shame for disappointing her, fear of admitting what I had done, and also, relief that I didn't have to carry this burden alone any longer.

That night my parents had a serious conversation with me about everything. I wouldn't tell them who the potential father was, partially because my dad kept eyeing his shotgun standing in the corner of his closet, but I did tell them that I'd only had sex one time, which was the truth. They repeatedly told me that obviously one time was enough. We talked about adoption and sending me away until the baby was born and all sorts of "pro-life" (pro-birth) options. They talked about the health and life of the baby. In the midst of all this I kept wondering, *What about* my *life?* While they talked I started daydreaming about suffering a major injury so the pregnancy would be over. I wondered whether getting super active in sports or taking a massive blow to the stomach area could spontaneously terminate a pregnancy. I wondered what would happen if I stopped eating. I wanted it all to go away. I didn't want a baby. I didn't want to be having this conversation. I wanted safety. Not only had I been traumatized from the actual act of having sexual intercourse, I was traumatized by the aftermath of the what-ifs and wonderings that came along with the condom falling off and a potential pregnancy. All I felt was shame. Sex was bad. I was bad. All of it was bad.

That night, at the end of all of the questions and crying and discussion, my mom hugged me and sent me to my room for bed. I didn't wonder about my mom's love. It was constant. I was so sad that I had disappointed her so greatly. But then my dad, the man whose face had been flushed and whose cheek had been twitching all evening over the news of his daughter's improper behavior and the potential consequences, gave me the biggest hug he'd ever given me. And while he wrapped his arms around me, he said words that I will never forget. "I love you. And no matter what, my love for you will never, ever end."

I cried myself to sleep that night ... not because of a baby, not because I had sex, not because of the shame I carried for myself and my family, but because of gratitude. I was so incredibly thankful that I knew that my dad (and mom) loved me. They loved me even though I jumped in the pool and had gone too far into the deep end. They loved me unconditionally and without question.

The next day I got my period. We never talked about it again.

On my dad's most recent birthday, he turned seventy-five. As of the date of this writing, he and my mom have eight grandchildren, three of whom are mine. He's probably quite pleased to know that those three magical creatures are karmically providing all the life lessons I need to learn and then some. And one of the biggest lessons we learn from each other every day is that in our family, we love each other, unconditionally. I encourage my kids to jump in and swim out into the deepend at every chance they get, while staying in earshot so I can help when they need me, no matter the circumstance, just like my parents did for me.

Happy birthday, Dad. I love you. And no matter what, my love for you will never, ever end.

BIG DICK ENERGY

→

Yes, you read that right: Big Dick Energy. My seventeen-year-old daughter used this phrase with me as I was embarking on my big road trip to somewhere south. She knew that I not only wanted, but I needed to spend time in self-care and reflection, see new things, and write this book. I laughed out loud and spun my head around and asked her what in the world she just said. "You've got Big Dick Energy, Mom, you're in control, you got this," she answered, maybe with a little too much confidence.

Huh. Big Dick Energy.

Sort of misogynistic and sort of hilarious. In the spirit of picking my battles, I chose to go with it.

My daughter is my hero. My she-ro. Since the day she was born she's been a fighter and a champion. She came out screaming and hasn't shut her beautiful mouth since. And I love it. She's amazing. She's a shepherd, not a sheep, and she does no harm but takes no shit. She recently came to the realization that adults are only just trying to figure out how to live life, and that there's no playbook, and that I wasn't lying when I told her that 80 percent of life is how you react to situations, because you only have control over one thing: yourself. She's sugar and spice and sparkle and fight, and I love her with all my being.

Equally amazing are her two brothers, and I love them with all my being, too. I've been accused of not loving my kids all the same.

That accusation is something I never have and never will receive. Questioning the depth of my love for my children is as hurtful as it is insulting. I love each of my children uniquely and fully with my entire heart and soul, and it shows up differently based on their personalities and their love languages. For example, I'll probably never take my daughter to the batting cages. I'll never coach her basketball team. But I do those things for my boys. I probably won't spend hours shopping with my boys, but I will wander the shops endlessly with my daughter. Loving my kids may not look the same, but I believe they know they are fully loved.

With the boys at their dad's for the week, and since our daughter lives with me full time, I took her to a vegan restaurant the day I began this road trip. She was born with a life-threatening dairy allergy, so it is a real treat when we find a place that is completely dairy-free and serves incredible food. Stated another way, *Eating without worrying about the risk of dying is a special treat.* No, it isn't lactose intolerance, and no, she hasn't outgrown it. Yes, she carries an EpiPen, and yes, she has had to use it. Being different can make you feel like an outsider no matter what that difference is, even if no one can see that difference. She has navigated her own journey of difference with remarkable grace, and I'm incredibly proud of her.

At age seventeen, she is on the cusp of so much adventure while simultaneously dancing on the outskirts of her childhood. She is in that magical space between little girl and woman, and every day gives her new opportunities to define herself and her life. It's both painful and amazing to experience this with her. I've watched her wrestle with her own darkness and light and, thankfully, her light has always won. Her light radiates from her, and everyone around her feels it. She doesn't fully know or understand that yet. I don't know if she understands how much gratitude I have that her soul chose mine to be her mom.

We talked about her plans and her dreams over our vegan lunch. She has some big things in store for her in the coming years. She's an incredible student and an all-star cheerleader. She plans to cheer for a Big Ten university. She wants to go premed. Her goals inspire the rest of us to do more. Her brothers adore her, and when they look at her they all shine like the sun and the moon. I love that they love each other. They are three pieces of my heart walking around outside my own body.

After we talked about her plans, she asked me about *my* goals and dreams. We talked about my need to travel in order to take care of myself and the concept for the book you're reading right now. She understood that part of who I am is my need to experience new places. She knew I was miserable in the latest iteration of my corporate career. She said she noticed that I've been a different person since my surgery and since being laid off, that the jolt has changed me ... for the better. Instead of saying to me, "Mom, you really need to get a real job," like others have said, her words were, "Mom, I am so proud of you for going after this. If anyone can do it, you can." She took a picture of me and Snapped it to her friends. My daughter told me she was proud of me—*and she even told her friends.* My eyes welled up with tears. I wrapped my arms and my red ribbon around her and held her tight with all the love of a mother's heart.

After I dropped her off at home I started my journey south. I had a framework of potential landmarks to see during my journey, starting with the Giant Lady's Leg Sundial in Roselawn, Indiana, which I had found on roadtrippers.com. I didn't do much research beyond that, I just knew it was a good stopping point to stretch and have a break from the drive, not too far off the freeway for me to visit. I drove for a few hours and soon approached my first stop. As I pulled up I noticed some security in place.

Interesting, a gated community, I thought to myself as I stepped out to stretch my legs. I walked up to the office and a young man greeted me. The office was more of a common area, and it looked like they had just thrown some kind of a party. Streamers were hanging from the ceiling. A few balloons and what looked like Mardi Gras beads were strewn about the room. The young man asked how he could help me, and I told him I was here to see the sundial.

He smiled and nodded. "Ah, the sundial." He yelled over his shoulder to a few people sitting across the room that he was taking a guest out to see the sundial, and they nonchalantly nodded in acknowledgment and carried on their conversation.

As we walked out the back of the office he asked me how I heard of the place. I explained the Roadtrippers website and that I was on a bit of a journey for myself, and also for a book. He seemed intrigued. We kept talking.

When I saw this place on the website, I knew I had to check it out. It seemed like a great icon in the Midwest that I had been missing all these years. I was surprised I had never heard of it before and that it seemed like such a secret. What I had failed to recognize was that the sundial was located inside a clothing-optional resort. I came to this realization as the young man told me that only he was authorized to take pictures to protect the privacy of the guests.

"If you want a picture, you need to give me your camera," he said.

That's when it hit me that I was actually inside the gates and on the grounds of a nudist resort. My immediate thought was, *My god, are they expecting me to take off my clothes?* Of course the answer was no, but funny that I immediately went to a place of anxiety and nervousness, and maybe even shame, at the thought of it.

He opened the door in the office and walked me out to the sundial. It was exactly what they said it was ... a giant Caucasian lady's leg, extended up and out with toes pointed due north, built off a wooden base that the young man described as a pageant-style walkway/stage for various resort events and traditions. Standing underneath it, my head came up to about mid-thigh. I wondered and giggled at the thought of what had gone on under and around this leg—if only this leg could talk, the stories it could tell!

My new friend took my picture (clothed) next to the silent and story-filled sundial, and I began to ask questions about the history of the resort. After some small talk, he offered me a full tour. I was surprised at his offer and immediately accepted, so we hopped in a golf cart and he gave me a full tour of the property. It seemed to be set up like a regular campsite with a tent area, cabins, and also more permanent, seasonal sites. The only difference was that many people there preferred to enjoy life in the nude. It was designed to be a full community, where people really got to know and care for each other. He suggested that, historically, there had been challenges, as one can imagine, but as of late there had not been any "issues." As a matter of fact while I was there, people were making plans about what time they were all attending church together. Based on my upbringing and understanding of the church, this was the last thing I expected to hear. My mind was absolutely blown.

I asked the young man how he came to work at a nudist resort and he explained he volunteered to join the team after his grandfather passed away and his parents acquired the business. He also mentioned that he grew up in the church and so he did not really know his grandfather because of his grandfather's "chosen lifestyle." I found it both Midwestern-typical and incredibly sad that assumptions around beliefs and taboos created these family barriers. When I asked him more about the history of the resort, all he would share was that some of the founding members had some wild stories to tell, and you wouldn't believe them if you heard them. I didn't take the time to meet or interview any of the founding members of the resort, as I felt like it really wasn't my place, but I would have loved to have talked to them. I felt like he had given me a glimpse into a secret society. I was fascinated.

After we exchanged pleasant goodbyes, I drove away thinking about how he had lost time with his grandfather over perceptions about lifestyle choices. I spent time thinking about how being raised in the church can prompt such shame around sexuality and non-marital, non-missionary, non-hetero sex. It made me sad to think about people being shunned because of who they are and the people they love. It also made me sad to think about how much shame we self-inflict in the name of conforming to religious and societal expectations that are laid on us, even with the best of intentions.

The entire experience made me think about my relationship with my kids and, someday, their kids. Although I already knew it in my heart, I spoke out loud a verbal commitment to *never* judge them or disown them or keep them from a family member because someone in the equation is a nudist. Or gay. Or trans. Or non-Lutheran. Or anything. I want them to know that just because someone does or is something different from what you know and who you are, it doesn't make that person bad. I want them to know that our differences are our superpowers. Those differences make us who we are and should be celebrated, not hidden. We may need interventions or therapy to help us correct harmful behaviors, but we don't need interventions or therapy to change who we are. What I want most for my children is for them to live their true and beautiful most authentic lives. I want them to discover themselves on their journeys in between their life milestones. I want them to love and be loved fully, without carrying the burden of shame.

That night I ended up in the Louisville area, and as I settled into my hotel room and finished the first day of my travels, I inhaled breaths of gratitude and paused to wander through my mind. I went back to the conversation I'd had with my daughter that morning. *She's proud of me for taking this journey. I hope the boys are proud of me, too. I am so incredibly proud of them.*

Then I laughed out loud remembering that, over lunch, she told me I have Big Dick Energy, and that somehow made it wildly appropriate that I had inadvertently wound up at a nudist resort. I thought about the young man and his grandfather, and it made me hope that my kids carried Big Dick Energy with them to wrestle out the darkness and to keep them bravely connected to all the important people in their world, even (and especially) on the hard days.

CAGED BIRDS

➤———→

I was using the restroom at Miguel's Pizza in Slade, Kentucky, and a man, without knocking, opened the door on me. I quickly said, "Almost done," and started to zip up my shorts when *another* person, a young girl, pushed the now partially open door open even farther, and then froze as she saw me. She quickly mumbled, "Sorry," and looked away. I laughed, trying to ease her obvious tension. It wasn't a big deal. This type of situation is par for the course in my world where weird and sometimes uncomfortable real-life things just tend to happen (like stopping to see a landmark and finding yourself a visitor in a nudist resort).

This place was a stop on my trip only because some people I met earlier in the day had told me about it. I was taking a morning hike in Cherokee Park when I passed two people talking and laughing. When the woman smiled and laughed, she radiated such incredible light and happiness that I knew I had to talk to them. I was nervous when I approached them, and they were welcoming. We had a great conversation, and at the end of our talk I asked if there was any place they'd recommend that I stop.

Without hesitation, the gentleman responded, "Red River Gorge, and definitely Miguel's Pizza." Because he answered so swiftly and definitively, I bailed on my other planned landmark visits and headed to Miguel's. The drive certainly did not disappoint. For nearly two hours I meandered through beautiful tree-lined Kentucky hills and carved rock valleys. I was listening to music by O.A.R., which is one of my favorites. At one point I got hooked on a line from their song "Caroline the Wrecking Ball": *You can never ground a bird that needs to fly.*

I replayed that part of the song over and over again during the drive. It's a great song with a great story. But that phrase kept replaying in my mind ... in some ways we all need to live like we're free. To fly. This was the first real summer since college that I'd experienced the freedom of not having a corporate job. I was savoring the feeling of having no place to go and anywhere to be. The summer sun and the conversations of the last two days and the open road and the music certainly had me feeling like I was flying. I was loving every second of being out of my day-to-day routine and, ultimately, in my element.

When I arrived at Miguel's Pizza I was able to order my slices how I wanted them—cheese pizza with extra fresh basil and white onions, and a freshly brewed, homemade sweet tea. As I was sitting at my picnic table, a woman walked by wearing a shirt that read ADVENTURER. DREAMER. BELIEVER. She smiled at me when she saw me admiring her shirt. I was immediately taken with this Bohemian spirit. I wanted to talk with her about freedom and adventures belonging to those who dreamed and believed. I watched for a moment to approach her and learn her story and also ask her where she got her shirt, but her boyfriend (husband?) seemed to want (demand) her full attention, so I stayed back. I decided her story wasn't meant to be part of mine that day, and I quietly observed from a distance. I did, however, notice that butterflies seemed to fly around and behind her as she walked. I know it was a coincidence they were there, but it seemed poetic and magical. *Adventurer. Dreamer. Believer.*

I waited for my pizza to come out and I thought about the freedom and possibility of adventuring and dreaming and believing. I was surprised when the darkness rose up strong in my mind. That darkness can be ugly and hate-filled, and sometimes sad and overwhelming. I started thinking about how we've been fed the line that the American dream was available for all people who worked hard and believed in the power of possibility. I thought about how, recently, people with significant leadership platforms seemed to be redesigning or simply disregarding the systems and rules of modern history that were designed to protect people. My two new friends from Cherokee Park summed it up quite nicely when they said that if you are complacent right now and not paying attention, it is most likely because the systems in place have been built to benefit you, or people who look like you. If you haven't personally felt the impact of what is going on, and if you aren't actively trying to make sure others have the same opportunities you have, that's an expression of privilege.

These profound words spoken by my young new friends gave me hope.

It was refreshing to hear the two of them discuss their perspectives on this topic. They shared the impact of their family and societal norms on their sociopolitical beliefs. They indicated how their international travel has influenced their worldview. The young woman even shared that her dad, who is a German citizen and legal resident, refuses to become an American citizen under someone like the current president of the United States (at the time of this writing, Donald Trump). Interestingly, she also mentioned that, because he looks like the majority of the people in power (white male) it would likely be much easier for her father to become a citizen than someone who has darker skin. We talked about how latent racism lives within the cultural fiber of our nation. We wondered if we, as a nation, would learn and heal from the reality of our history.

As we talked, they mentioned that they were both heading back to college in the coming days. I asked them what I should share with my kids, especially my daughter, since she will be starting college soon. Their responses varied. Her first response was to find your community and stick with them. *(Find your tribe!)* In her first days on campus she had found friends in the Greek system who became her people, her safety net. His opinion was a bit different, because he wasn't confident that typical Greek life traditions consistently offered safety as a priority for young women. I noted the perspective in their opinions based on gender, and found it interesting. The young woman's next comments were to study abroad if at all possible. She explained that her international travels really opened her up to hear and understand how members of our global society perceived the current status of the United States.

Her exact words were, "They are laughing at us."

Sad.

The young man talked about a trip he had taken to Nairobi as a photojournalist. He said that the intentions of the trip were good, but, as they say, the road to hell is paved with good intentions. I asked him what he meant by that specifically, and he explained that these quick trips of two weeks at a time to help a certain group in a certain nation with a certain problem are incredible gestures, until you start to peel back the layers of the onion. Western colonization has had a largely negative impact on the systems and cultures of non-Western societies and communities over hundreds of years. He described how the two-week Band-Aid fix does nothing to challenge the underlying systemic issues that some nations face as a result of Western power and politics. We have created crises in nations and now we claim that only we can fix them. The Western colonial Jesus has arrived to save you!

All their comments and perspectives reinforced for me the importance of global awareness and international travel so that we all can have a better understanding of our roles within our global existence. I made a mental note to make sure I'm encouraging my kids to be appreciative of experiences over things so they can learn to be aware of themselves and their environments and the impacts they have on others, in their families, their communities, and their world.

Our conversation turned to the family-separation policies and the scary state of affairs at the border. We talked about the need for compassion and how scary it must be for the children who were taken from their parents and put into cages. We wondered out loud about who was helping these children. We talked about the short attention span of Americans, and how it was possible that these children might eventually be forgotten. The young man mentioned that his friend's dad was recently detained by ICE and that another friend was living in a constant state of fear for undocumented family members.

The government certainly has its work cut out for it in figuring out a compassionate and humane solution to the challenges faced by a global society. As humans we have our work cut out for *us* to figure out how to not turn a blind eye to the inhumane treatment of children at the border and individuals of all ages, races, religious beliefs, and sexual orientation, all across our nation and the world.

During the acute phase of my surgery recovery earlier this year, I met a group of people on Twitter who unexpectedly became my friends. Even though we'd never met in person, these people became part of my tribe. There is one woman in our group whose church recently did some active humanitarian work with refugees at the border. She sent this e-mail about her experiences (shared with her permission):

> *Yesterday I spent all day preparing to receive a busload of refugees from Guatemala. This was my first time to do this work. When they arrived, the clergy committee met them on the bus and said a prayer. Once they were inside awaiting intake, we greeted each family and told them, "Welcome to Dallas. You are no longer detained. You are free." Everyone was crying, except this one very serious young man, all of five or six years old. He just sat there, looking everyone over, surveying the scene, occasionally putting a protective hand on his mom. He looked like a fifty-year-old. All were sunbaked. Most were in pretty good health. One kid showed up with the flu. Another infant arrived with a 104-degree fever. That family was immediately taken to the hospital. On the whole, it was very rewarding but equally heartbreaking. There were so many children, y'all ... sooo many kids. If everyone in this country did this work for just one day, I bet we'd be having a lot fewer talks about walls. We'll be doing this all summer, helping two buses per week of folks get to their families here.*

She has inspired our Twitter group with her work, and she has demonstrated the beauty of compassion. This woman has shown me what Jesus really looks like. *Whatever you did for the least of these, you did for me. (Matthew 25:40).*

I have a relative who said to me, "But why are they coming here?" Oh, I don't know ... maybe the same reason your great-grandparents came here. Perhaps, like my new friends in the park discussed, some of the families seeking asylum in the United States are experiencing social and political unrest because Western governments and political greed have disrupted the systems that may have otherwise protected them. And when they arrived, they found that all of our policies and procedures, imperfect as they were, were thrown out the window in exchange for indefinite family separation, detention, and overcrowded cages.

The issue isn't just about politics. Immigration is about real people and real lives. It's an issue of compassion and humanity. Our response to family separation policies speaks to our empathy and defines our character. How we treat our fellow human beings is the core of who we are.

The government of the United States is putting children in cages, and those kids are getting sick and dying in custody, without their parents and away from their families. Those children are experiencing a major life jolt at an early age, and they have no freedom or power to control or change their situation. This, sadly, at the hands of the government of freedom, is their life in between. Their lives will forever be defined by their pre-caged time, and their time after internment. This is darkness. This is pain. These children need healing.

The silence of those not directly impacted by this humanitarian crisis is deafening. Their willingness to turn a blind eye to these children is an act of complicity in turning the key in the locks on the cages.

As I sat at the outdoor pizza and rock climbing place in Kentucky, I was sickened by the inhumanity and cruelty of putting actual children in cages. I watched the woman with the adventurers. dreamers. believers. shirt, still talking with her husband. I wondered about the dreams of the kids and their parents, and I wondered what adventures they had given up on, and if they had dreams left to believe in. I imagined the atrocities they escaped and the risks they took. I wondered if they still believed in the promise that is America. I pictured how fast their smiles and tears of joy turned to pain and devastation when they were torn away from the loving arms of their mothers. I wondered if they understood why they were being treated as criminals. Hell I wondered if *I* understood why they were being treated as criminals! I thought about how America's collective attention span is being pulled from one atrocity to the next, and I was horrified to think about how we have largely forgotten about them.

As compassionate humans, we should be helping all children spread their wings so they can fly, not clip them and build systems that seek to oppress them for pursuing the dream of freedom.

I was surprised at the weight of my sadness. I was free, on the road and adventuring. But I was also painfully aware. I sipped my sweet tea. I looked at the woman with the shirt. I thought about the children in cages. I was angry. I felt physically sick. I wondered how a divided America could possibly heal from the damage of these most recent years of normalized racism and greed.

You can never ground a bird that needs to fly … The line from that song played again in my mind. I thought about those kids. We shouldn't ground them or cage them. We should hear their stories and honor them. We should learn about their dreams. We should celebrate the things that make them unique, even if it's different than who and what we are. We should give them an entry point to the freedom of which they dream. These kids need to fly, and it is our job to compassionately help them and offer healing.

What you would want for your own child?

HEY, MISSOURI

>>————→

When I first started talking about this road trip and the idea for this book, my Pinterest feed began to fill with pictures of Asheville, North Carolina. I had heard of Asheville before, but I didn't know much about it. Pinterest made it seem like a progressive hotbed of art and music, a cultural haven for Bohemian spirits. I liked the idea, and I like when the Universe gives me signs, so I decided to drive in that general direction.

As I drove through the beautiful countryside I couldn't help but wonder about the broad diversity of our country and our communities. Growing up in the Midwest gives me a specific Midwestern perspective (and accent, according to some). People who grow up out east or out west typically have different experiences and points of view. As I was on the road, stopping at gas stations, witnessing interactions, I wondered about the people I saw and what made us all alike as well as what made us different. I wondered what stories went untold between all of us.

The sun was setting and I was still an hour or so outside of Asheville, so I spent a few minutes finding a hotel for the night. I figured I would do a quick check-in somewhere, find a place to grab a bite to eat, log in and do some writing, and then get a good night's sleep.

The Universe had other plans for me. I found a Days Inn that fit my search criteria and booked it quickly so I could keep driving. When I put the hotel address in the GPS, it took me right around Asheville and about ten miles west of the city. I watched the city disappear over my shoulder as I drove into the fading sunlight and decided to just roll with whatever was in store. I pulled into the parking lot of the Days Inn lobby, got out of the car, stretched, and walked up the stairs. When I got inside, the woman at the front desk was helping a woman who had arrived what seemed to be just moments before me.

I have done quite a bit of traveling for work, and for those who have been road warriors, there is a distinct difference between traveling for business and traveling for pleasure. When I'm alone and on business (read: no kids with me), I walk with purpose, don't check bags, complete online check-ins, stand on the right and walk on the left, exchange pleasantries with people but keep small talk to a minimum, move swiftly, and quite frankly just get things done. When I traveled routinely for work, people in terminals started to become familiar. I often saw the husband of one friend en route in the terminal in Atlanta on Tuesdays, where we exchanged a quick nod hello and maybe a comment about the kids while walking to different gates for different destinations. A group of the same people traveled from the same terminal on Tuesday mornings, and even though we were all strangers and no one spoke to each other, we became familiar simply by our schedules and patterns.

The difference in this journey was that even though I was traveling alone and sort of for work, it was anything but transactional and quick. There was no travel routine, no familiar faces, and no particular destination.

The woman in front of me in the lobby was filling out paperwork for her hotel room. Actual paperwork. With a pen. The lady behind the desk was drawing out a map, on paper, with a pen, of where we were and where the woman should drive to park in front of her room. She explained the breakfast hours and menu in great detail, and her words rolled out with a Southern accent, thick and long. She explained that she was particularly fond of the biscuits and gravy and highly recommended them. My stomach growled. The check-in for the lady in front of me lasted about fifteen minutes longer than anticipated. I was hungry and getting impatient. As they finally wrapped up the check in, I heard the traveler say she had Missouri plates on her car and that she was only staying for one night. I kept looking at the time on my phone. It was late. I gave up on having dinner for the evening.

It was now my turn to check in and I prepared myself to hear the same rehearsed speech about the map and the breakfast menu and the biscuits and gravy. I gave the associate my credit card and my driver's license so she could write down the numbers, with a pen, on whatever papers she had in front of her.

As she did that, the lady who checked in before me came back into the lobby asked me, "Hey, do you know anything about cars? I can't get my dome light turned out and I don't want the battery to die."

I looked at her and said, "Did you google it? Do you have a handbook? If the button doesn't work I'm not sure what to tell you."

I probably could have been more helpful, but I was caught off guard. I was tired and hungry, and my acute stress disorder was kicking in. I recognized it. Within seconds my mind had irrationally concocted the idea that she was trying to get me into her car to knock me out and kidnap or rob me. This traveler from Missouri was petite, and I'm fairly tall, so I knew I shouldn't be worried about my physical safety, but I felt anxious nonetheless. Once I calmed myself enough to be rational, I made a note that I needed to rewire my brain to not be so afraid all the time.

I finished signing in three places and wrote down the information from my Wisconsin plates. I thanked the woman behind the desk, took my old-school room key from 1984 and went back to my car. I had to drive uphill to my room. When I got out, I turned to look across the parking lot. The moon was shining brightly and the silhouette of the tree-lined mountains pressed up against the night sky. It was beautiful. I paused and took a deep breath in, thankful for the beauty and the adventure. The night air smelled like freedom.

I grabbed my backpack out of my back seat and turned to go into my room. A car with Missouri plates was parked a few spots down. I figured it was the lady who checked in before I did. Her car was packed to the gills, and it looked like her dome light was off. I began to silently reprimand myself for feeling nervous about her while simultaneously wondering why her car was packed to overflowing. I convinced myself that she was running away from an abusive relationship, changing her identity, and starting over with a new life somewhere in the beautiful South. I fell asleep while entertaining random fictional plot lines.

The next morning I got myself ready and stepped outside. The mountains were just as majestic against the morning sky as they were in the pale moonlight. I inhaled deeply and whispered words of gratitude. My stomach interrupted me by growling. Loudly. I tossed my backpack in my car and drove down to the lobby for breakfast. I was planning to eat the biscuits and gravy and then go to the Biltmore Estate and maybe into downtown Asheville for the afternoon. When I walked into the breakfast lobby I saw the woman with the dome light problems sitting alone at a table toward the front of the room. "Hey Missouri," I called out as I approached her. She seemed to startle when I approached. I wondered if she had acute stress disorder, too. I tried to reassure her by smiling when she looked up at me. "Did you get your light fixed?"

She seemed to relax for a moment and smiled back. She proceeded to tell me that she figured out her light and that she, too, was planning on going to the Biltmore for the day. She asked what I was traveling for and I explained the loose concept of the book. She seemed interested. She told me she had just had some significant family changes, and that she was a lawyer headed to Washington, D.C., for work. *I knew it!* I thought to myself. *She's escaping her abuser and starting over!* I told her it was nice to meet her and I wished her good luck and a safe journey. I walked through the buffet line to get some biscuits and gravy, and I sat down in the back of the room to eat my breakfast. After a few moments, Missouri approached me and told me that her passion was screenplays, and that she wanted to keep in touch about the book. We exchanged Facebook information. She was leaving for the Biltmore. I told her maybe I'd see her later on that day. Since we were leaving at different times, I didn't expect to see her again.

I finished my breakfast and watched the news. I watched the same woman at the front desk move methodically through her paperwork and smile and talk to the guests who came in for breakfast. Everyone seemed connected, even though some were coming and some were going. I was curious about people's stories and wondered about why and where they were traveling.

My mind wandered as I drove away from the hotel. Ten minutes or so passed, and I pulled up to the Biltmore Estate parking lot. I immediately saw my new friend walking toward the ticket area. *All right, Universe, I see what you're trying to do here.* I shook my head and laughed. This woman wasn't a kidnapper, and she actually probably wasn't a battered woman escaping some awful situation. She was a wanderer, like me. She was going through some major life changes and for her it made sense to pick up and move across the country, just like for me it made sense to take myself camping or go on a road trip to reset and center myself. We both were traveling for our own self-care and to feed our wandering souls ... existing in other places so that we could remember who we were and then come home to ourselves. I found a parking spot, got out of my car, and yelled out to her, "Hey Missouri!" She turned around and smiled. We chatted for a bit and decided to do the tour together.

If you haven't been to the Biltmore, it's a must-see. It's absolutely beautiful. Grandiose. Breathtaking. I did hear someone call it a "monument to excess," and while that description is somewhat fitting, I'm also reminded that not only is it historically fascinating, it also employs I believe 2,700-ish people, which is really incredible. As we wandered through the massive property and never-ending rooms, we made jokes about "Professor Plum with the rope in the library!"

Over the course of the day we had deep conversations about family and relationships and politics and dating in our forties. We discussed the blessing and the curse of being accomplished adult women who had to endure the overwhelming burden of student loans while balancing traditional societal pressures as well as professional expectations. We talked about being athletes and recovering from injuries, how our bodies are built to endure so much, but also take time to heal. We talked about our extended healing times due to our age. Even though we just met, and even though we had completely different upbringings and experiences, I could see so much of her in me and me in her. Our red ribbon began to wrap around us, and it grew stronger with every story we exchanged.

Since we both had a love of current events, we talked politics. We talked women's rights. We talked human rights. We talked about the kids in cages. We talked about racism. Over the course of the day, we discussed conflict resolution and mediation, something both of us were trained in and passionate about. We shared details about our most recent dating and relationship experiences. We talked about men who claim to be all for civil rights, but after a few weeks or months they begin to show their true colors with their racist jokes and/or subtle intolerance of intelligent women.

We vehemently agreed that those traits warranted a full stop.

We toured the estate, we walked the gardens, and we eventually went to sample some of the Biltmore wines. We offered each other work and relationship advice, relating to each other's search for love while managing bills and navigating the pressures of adult life. As the tour wound down, we both realized our time together was soon coming to an end. When I asked what she was doing next she said she was headed off to D.C. She said she needed to be there by next week Tuesday. I asked if she wanted to go into downtown Asheville and grab lunch; I promised to only keep her for a few hours so she had plenty of time to make her journey to D.C. She agreed.

We sat outdoors at Tupelo Honey and enjoyed a leisurely patio lunch while chatting the afternoon away. Missouri explained that she was expecting to fall into a job pretty quickly based on some old connections from D.C. We talked about her passion for writing screenplays and daydreamed about what we might accomplish collaboratively. We entertained ideas of creating short films. We talked about honoring our own passions and true selves. I told her she should ditch the guy she was considering dating. She told me that I might meet someone really special someday. It was refreshing to have a conversation about all these topics with no judgment. All we had was a sincere appreciation for each other.

As our lunch came to a close, we started to say our goodbyes. This seemingly random encounter with a like-minded soul had taken on great meaning to me throughout the day, and I wanted to somehow celebrate our meeting. I asked her if she wanted to go get a piercing or a tattoo or something to commemorate our experience. She told me she wasn't in a position to do that, job search and all. I understood her position completely, but I decided I might still do something of that nature. She told me that if I was ever in D.C. I should be in touch and that I could always stay with her. I told her that if she's in Milwaukee she should do the same. We hugged and that red ribbon wrapped around us and promised to bind us together no matter our distance. I was thankful the Universe brought us together. The friendship we found and the memories we created that day were made up of adventuring magic and pure joy.

She drove away, and I spent the next few hours wandering the downtown area, in and out of shops. Eventually I came across a tattoo shop and got my nose pierced, both to commemorate my memory of the day and to serve as a small act of disobedience to the corporate culture in which I had felt trapped for so long.

I paused and I breathed in the freedom of the moment. I silently smiled and offered up a prayer of gratitude for my new friend and for the day of conversation. I realized that, even after the chaos of life had jolted me again and again, Happiness still, somehow, found me. Even when I was unrecognizably trapped in my own madness, Happiness still showed up, encouraging me to accept myself in all my imperfection. Happiness whispered in my ear that she had been there silently, waiting for me ... that I was worthy of her ... and she promised that, even on her quiet days, she would never, ever leave.

Then Happiness wrapped me up in sunlight and magic and nudged me further on my journey. I hopped in my car and kept on driving. Unbeknownst to me, I was going home to good friends.

"FRAMILY"

$\longrightarrow$

ater that night I arrived at my friends' home in Waxhaw, North
Carolina. We used to be neighbors. Our daughters attended elementary school together. Their jobs took them out of state about
four years prior. I am acquainted with a lot of people, and I have a lot
of friendships, but within my own neighborhood, there are very few
people with whom I share a close connection. Brett and Lisa, my old
neighbors, are two of the very best people I know.

One of my favorite memories of them as my neighbors took place
on an early summer evening. I was busy straightening the house and
straightening my life when my phone rang. I saw Lisa's name and
immediately picked up. "Heeeyyyy, how's it going?"

We chatted for a minute and she asked if I was busy that evening.
I said that I wasn't, and a second later the doorbell rang. I told her to
hold on because someone was at the door. I wasn't really expecting
anyone, and when I looked out the window next to the front door, I
saw both Brett and Lisa, Lisa still with phone in hand. I opened the
door surprised and confused. I welcomed them in; they had called
from my front porch prepared for an impromptu gathering with a few
bottles of wine and some snacks. At that point, my divorce was still
pretty fresh, and I was trying to understand how our post-divorce
friendships were sorting out. I had been feeling quite isolated, so
this was a very welcome surprise. I didn't know how much I needed
to just kick back with my friends. More importantly, I didn't realize

the incredible and genuine friendship I had with them. That evening, over a few glasses (bottles) of wine, I was reminded what true and unconditional friendship felt like. It was exactly what I needed. They were my tribe.

The same unconditional friendship feelings happened during my road trip visit. I knew I wanted to head this general direction when I started driving, but I didn't have any set plans. I saw on social media that Brett and Lisa were visiting family in Michigan, and I didn't know what date I would arrive anywhere, so I hadn't told them or anyone, really, where I would be. I texted their daughter (one of my daughter's best friends and whom I love as my own child) and asked if they had enjoyed Michigan and when they were coming home. She replied that they were already back.

Before I could even answer her message, Lisa texted me, *So I heard a rumor.*

I responded, *Haha what's that?*

Are you really coming to visit? Lisa replied. I figured Hannah had found me on the Snap Map and knew I was in North Carolina.

> Me: *Well, if you happen to be around, I could be in the area. :)*

> Lisa: *Sure. Just let me know for how long? And what time.*

> Me: *I know it's ridiculously late notice so no worries if not.*

> Lisa: *We love visitors. I can work from home on Tuesday if it is early.*

> Me: *Probably would be late Tuesday and would leave early Thursday morning if that works. I was going to call you tonight when I figure out where I'm staying.*

> Lisa: *Ok are you not staying with me because you hate me? We have plenty of room and a Hannah.*

Me: *I'm driving so I won't get there until Tuesday. Can
I stay with you those two nights? Because I love you <3.*

Lisa: *Absolutely. I insist.*

This is how I know I am with my tribe. Not only did they insist I stay with them when there was absolutely no notice, they prepared for my visit and made me feel as if I belonged with them. They had a message written on the mirror in the bathroom I used, as well as eye makeup remover, face moisturizer, and eye pads to reduce puffiness set out for me to use when I arrived. Further, they encouraged me to stay three nights instead of the proposed two, Lisa called in to work so we could hang out, and on the third night when additional friends came to stay they welcomed all of us with a big dinner and flowing wine, amazing conversation, and overall good vibes. They took care of me. Even though I had never been in their new house, I felt completely at home.

On one of the days I was there, Brett and I were discussing careers and our similar experience of being in "vocational purgatory." We both were in situations where workplace "transformations" made lay-offs imminent, leaving us both feeling unsteady, questioning our next steps, optimistic about opportunities but concerned about economic constraints. While our work and overall life situations were quite different, the harsh reality of falling victim to corporate restructuring was a commonality that allowed for significant bonding. To a certain extent, I found myself in his situation, and he found himself in mine. What was a stark difference, however, was the partnership Brett and Lisa had, and how they were navigating together. As Brett was planning his next career moves based on ever-changing circumstances, Lisa was planning her next moves based on their collaborative vision and plans. I listened to them talk about the opportunities and options, pros and cons, travel requirements, and overall expectations of how they would handle new opportunities. I loved listening to them run their ideas by each other with admiration and sarcasm and wit and grace. I admired their partnership, and I wondered if I'd ever experience having a teammate-in-life.

I am filled with gratitude that I got them in my divorce.

Looking back a few years, Brett and Lisa were also the people who stayed at my house, outside, until I got home, after discovering that I had been robbed. This was the first time I was robbed, not the time we came back from Disney. I had been traveling in Newport Beach for work and didn't think much about being gone. The kids were with their dad and they had activities to do, so I simply compartmentalized my work and family life and built systems to make sure things went on according to plan. I was not expecting a call from my daughter, who was thirteen at the time, that afternoon.

"Mom, where are you?" I was happy to hear her sweet voice, but alarmed to sense her concern.

I answered, "I just got back from Newport Beach. I'm running a few errands and then I'll be home. Why?"

"There's a hole in the patio door," she said.

"What did you say?"

"Mom, there's a hole in the patio door. I'm here with Hannah because we're doing a neighborhood scavenger hunt and there's a hole in the back door."

"Don't go inside," I tried to say calmly. "Call Hannah's mom and dad and go to the neighbor's house." My heart was pounding. I didn't know if there had been a storm or a break-in. I didn't know if she and Hannah were in danger. My kids were with their dad while I was traveling, but obviously my daughter was there now. I drove to my home in a complete panic.

I don't remember exactly how everything happened next, but by the time I got home, Brett and Lisa were already there, not only keeping the kids calm, but talking to the police and the neighbors about the situation. My tribe was there … handling things for me until I arrived, and then handling things *with* me until I could stand on my own. The police went into the house to make sure no one was still inside, and I remember being partially scared, partially confused, partially in absolute disbelief. After the police ensured that the house was clear, we went inside to find that it had been a "smash and grab" job, most of the valuables and collectibles stolen, but no major damage had been done beyond that. The thieves had thrown a brick through the patio door, and the brick had torn up the linoleum across the dining area, but that was about it for physical damages. The emotional damage was much more devastating.

Not knowing if you are safe in your own home can throw off everything else in your world. Feelings of not being safe lead to lack of sleep which can lead to extraordinary stress. Stress, left unmanaged, can impact your physical health, and potentially affect your ability to seek and retain employment. In our culture, we preach self-resilience and tell people to pull themselves up by their bootstraps, and this messaging can sometimes cause us to become so fiercely independent that it becomes harmful. We get so busy being strong, we wall ourselves off from our friends and self-isolate in order to prove we are strong and resilient enough to survive. Once we lose connections, our self-esteem and sense of self-preservation can crumble, leaving feelings of helplessness and hopelessness. It is impossible to dream when you're in survival mode. And it can be a vicious, vicious cycle.

That night and for the following weeks, I didn't sleep much at all. I startled at the slightest noise and felt as if I was constantly on guard. I tried to sort out the paperwork for the detectives and the insurance company but it felt like a never-ending battle. My friends and family helped with the cleanup of broken glass and repair of the patio door. As much as they were able, they made sure I was okay. I tried to stay strong and be resilient and put on the appearance that I was okay, but I felt infinitely violated.

When I look back on the day of the robbery and the immediate aftermath, I am fully aware of the role that Brett and Lisa played, and I will be forever thankful. Not only did they show up when, again, I didn't know I needed them, but they stayed to make sure everything was going to be okay.

And now, on this road trip, after having my life massively interrupted through surgery and a layoff, I didn't know how much I needed to just *be* with them. I didn't know how much I needed to feel like I was at home with my people. I needed them so much that I stayed for three days. They welcomed me with open arms, even though I was unannounced and unexpected. They took care of me. Brett and Lisa have become my family ... my "framily" ... and no matter the time or distance between us, we will have each other. They are my tribe. Sometimes you realize that it doesn't matter where you are, that it's who you're with that creates your home. Without knowing it, in so many big and small ways, Brett and Lisa have led me toward the light so I could come home to myself.

PROTECT YOUR PEACE

$\longrightarrow$

There's no easy pathway to healing from past experiences and past wounds, especially when reminders get kicked up in day-to-day conversations, news cycles, and, sadly, new traumas. The pathway to becoming whole can be messy and dark. Sometimes healing only happens when you're forced into it.

Healing and self-care are not to be confused with self-maintenance. Manicures and massages have been marketed as self-care, when really they are tools for maintaining our health and beauty amid cultural norms and professional expectations. Self-care is soul work. Self-care is living your life unapologetically with fierce authenticity. Self-care is taking the time to consciously acknowledge and celebrate differences. Self-care is surrounding yourself with people who will love you and challenge you and take care of you (your tribe!). Self-care is removing those who do not, and who would not. Wisdom and growth and healing come from learning the difference.

Being forced to slow down after a major jolt can throw your entire nervous system into a panic. In one moment, everything can change. The exact moment the bone breaks, or the anesthesia takes hold, or the separation paperwork is handed to you, your entire world as you know it flips upside down. And instead of going a mile a minute to accomplish everything, you are finally forced to stop, analyze yourself, reposition yourself for major changes, and start all over again.

In our culture, we are conditioned from early on to engage in the rat race of life. Supposedly we must work harder to climb and achieve the next level and the next degree and do more and be bigger, better, faster, stronger! But seldom have we been trained to sit in our own calm and in our silence, to simply *be*. We don't take time to remember who we were or to discover who we have actually become, but we need to do just that. When we get jolted, we *change*. Our brains rewire themselves. Our old muscles atrophy as we learn to flex the new ones. Our identities become modified in subtle and not-so-subtle ways. For example, I am still athletic, but I'm not the athlete I once was. I am still a hard worker, but my goals related to my career have changed. I am still a mom, but my kids need me differently now than they did when they were infants/toddlers. I am still a believer, but the way I believe faith in action actually works is quite different from what I memorized in confirmation (brainwashing) class. I still want a partner, but I want a partner differently than I did in my twenties. I don't want someone who wants to have babies and do Disney every other year. I want a partner who not only matches me intellectually and physically and spiritually today, but is committed to growing and changing together for the rest of our lifetime. I want someone who wants to jump into the deep end of the pool holding hands so we can swim together.

I want the seeds in our souls to blossom into beautiful flowers in the garden we create together, nurtured with attention and love and patience and time.

Time alone and time away gives you the opportunity to really dig in and think about your connections and your relationships. Over time, "What did I do wrong?" gives way to "What should I do differently?" and "Have I learned what I needed to learn?" I don't want to get stuck on that river of life, getting handed those same lessons to learn over and over again. No one gives twenty years to an employer expecting to get laid off. No one goes out to play a sport expecting to end up in the hospital. No one goes into marriage expecting to get divorced, yet that's where so many of us end up.

Being alone is both a devastating and empowering experience. On the journey of single adult survival, my girlfriend and I have started asking each other "What's the worst thing that could happen?" That question alone has helped both of us learn to make courageous decisions on our own.

Many of my divorced friends have found themselves in new relationships quickly, some even getting married what seemed to be shortly after their breakups. Personally I've often wondered whether I really want to get married again, or if there's something about me that has prevented me from having a long-lasting relationship and partnership. I remember one time typing on my laptop, *Do you want to be in a relationship again?* I stared at that line in silence for what seemed like a very long time, the emotionless black letters typed out on the sterile white screen. It felt like a stare down, the light wrestling the dark right there on the paper in front of me, not sure if "good" or "bad" was assigned to either light or dark, yes or no. After several minutes of squinting angrily at my computer screen, I typed, *YES!* and shut my laptop hard and fast. Only several weeks later did I reopen that document and dive into what that actually meant. My ex-husband had someone living with him. Did that mean that the timeline was right for me to start dating? I had no clue what to do. I still wasn't sure what I had learned. I still hadn't given my soul seeds all the care and nurturing they needed. I wasn't ready to share a garden with anyone. I was still trying to figure out what kind of flowers I could bloom on my own.

I had no clue how to grow my own garden. I felt like I was on indefinite pause from my divorce and from the word-wounds that echoed in my mind. I was in a very dark place, and no flowers were going to bloom without sunlight. There was a void. I was missing companionship. I was missing having a partner in life. I was learning how to let the sunshine in. I talked to my therapist. I spent time with the good friends who emerged and offered to stand by my side. I started doing yoga and working out more intentionally. I usually made healthy choices to encourage the light to come through a little bit more. And then there were the times I thought I was being hard-core and joked about drinking the extra glass (bottle) of wine, where I took the extra pain meds because it eased my tension and helped me sleep. I wasn't slowing down to sit in my own silence and learn who I was as a changed person ... I was planning massive exercise plans to achieve some monumental accomplishment that had the potential to destroy my body. Somehow I thought that this was the way to fill the void when really what I needed to do was to be still, remember who I was, and take the long journey into myself to decide who I wanted to be.

My recently divorced girlfriend and I have been having this conversation for the last few years. She has shared with me the very relatable circumstances of her post-divorce loneliness. The overwhelming sense of being alone has kicked up feelings of unworthiness, compounded by ongoing emotional trauma related to the aftermath of divorce. Even those of us who believe we are built strong and can handle anything can be emotionally beaten to a pulp. No one really knows because they can't see it hidden behind our smiles. Our therapists might know, but only if we've been brave enough to share. Unworthiness in the time of a "pause" is a dark and dangerous feeling, and most flowers don't bloom in the dark.

We talked about how, during periods of loneliness and darkness, receiving attention feels good. It's a self-esteem booster and helps fill the void left by the emotional pain, and it can be addictive. But it often comes with shame. My girlfriend shared that she has been receiving advances from a friend, a married man, who shares dick pics and talks dirty behind the comfort and safety of his smartphone.

Translation: There's no real intimacy involved. It's safe. It's harmless. It's instant gratification and it's pure pleasure. For him. It's completely unfair to his wife (unless, of course, they have some sort of arrangement). So what do you do? If you respond it's an assumed agreement to engage. If you don't respond, you're somehow a bitch for not responding, or you will damage his ego and your friendship by ignoring the situation. But now, even though the advances are unsolicited and unprompted, the burden is carried by the receiver, not the sender. After the messages eventually pause or stop, there's relief ... but the void and the unworthiness return, because now you've offended a friend by not responding the way he wanted, and it's lonely. This creates a downward and overwhelmingly vicious spiral.

This is a multifaceted, complex issue that's not easily solved, but it is important to address because it's not uncommon. It happens all the time. Maybe not the same players with the same roles, but unwanted electronic sexual advances are likely here to stay. If we don't at least call it out, name it, and claim it, the shame will keep coming along with the messages, the void won't be healed, and the lesson will never be learned. And when you're already in darkness or looking for validation, it's easy to get sucked in. It's easy to engage or blow it off or make light of it. When we don't set boundaries, it's bound to happen again.

Somewhere on the drive between the Big Pencil in Wytheville, Virginia, and Hillbilly Hot Dogs in Lesage, West Virginia, my girlfriend and I discussed this topic, at length. We had joked about the situation before, but it wasn't until we actually dug into it that we realized we were experiencing some of the same feelings. After we figured out what we knew and didn't know about our own internalized patterns of unworthiness, we decided, in a spirit of openness and without judgment, that there are a few guidelines that could prove useful:

1. Recognize what is and is not tolerable behavior from a friend or a partner, and that sending dick pics is a pretty good indication that this dude just wants to screw you, and isn't looking for an actual long-term partnership. This might be okay in some consensual relationships, but in some, it isn't. It's important to recognize the difference.

2. Reclaiming your power and setting new boundaries is crucial to making sure the darkness and the void, which will inevitably be there at different points in life, are filled with good things that you choose and allow, rather than the nonsense that shows up by default, or by the choice of someone else who is simply looking for instant gratification. It is okay to say no, and it is okay if a

decision you make angers others. It is not your job to fix others or keep them happy.

3. Another powerful part of this process is forgiveness. Forgiving ourselves for our past mistakes and decisions, and no longer taking on shame for the choices and behaviors of someone else, is mission critical to moving out of the darkness. Again, this is no easy task, and it takes time and meditation and practice. If you're in a period of darkness, it can be particularly hard work, but this active forgiveness is precisely the type of self-care that needs to be practiced to give the light a fighting chance to win.

4. You are responsible for you and no one else. You have a right to your own feelings, and your emotions are valid. You are enough as you are, and you don't need to change yourself for anyone but you.

There is much more at play here than the interactions between adults. This issue of the expectations in relationships and partnerships is made even more complex by additional societal forces, including familial assumptions, religious guilt, and overall social norms. For women, there are pressures to be pretty enough but not too pretty, to look young enough to be desirable but not immature, sexy enough but not too sexual, strong enough but not too strong that no man would want to take care of you.

As if this wasn't complicated enough, layer in the dick pics and the shame of decisions past and the effort it takes to focus on healing, and it's no wonder that it just seems easier to keep coming up with workout plans and drinking wine. How is anyone supposed to find an actual relationship when there's all this pressure? Sometimes my girlfriends and I laugh and wonder if we should bother to date at all, especially when it seems that not everyone is playing by the same rules.

The good news is that there is relief in talking through these real-life adult pressures. Once my girlfriends and I got vulnerable and shared our thoughts and experiences, we found more commonalities across our stories. Despite our differences, we're all having similar internal dialogues regarding cultural expectations and norms; we're all holding onto shame from not meeting the expectations of our families and our churches and our friends; we're all struggling with what the hell to do with the unsolicited dick pics! Through our conversations, we have started shedding some of that shame, healing our souls from past traumas, and moving toward living our most authentic lives.

In action, the work of self-care and healing brings about hard decisions. It shows up in releasing, without apology, those who are not honoring boundaries. For me, it is important to be the guardian of my own experience and the garden of my heart. I've begun to say no to people and things that are not serving me in both my personal and professional space, and I've grown in my expectation that others will do the same. When people are in my home, whether family or friend, comments that I believe are inappropriate or non-inclusive are addressed as gracefully as possible. My boundaries are set to ensure that my values are honored in my home and in my space.

It's an imperfect journey filled with missteps, but every decision made in alignment with our own values is a step in the right direction, and it brings a sense of empowerment and peace. It's easy to keep people close who are willing to respect boundaries. With practice, it gets easier to remove people who refuse to show the same respect. Over time, it becomes second nature to protect your peace.

Listening to and building up the women in our lives who are learning to reset their boundaries is important, because *empowered women empower women*. We need to wrap each other in the red ribbons of friendship and love and remind each other that we aren't alone. I'm going to pour light on my girlfriends so their gardens can grow by spending more time reminding them they are brilliant, they are beautiful, and they're worthy of love, whether it be self-love, the love of friends, the love of a companion, or the love of a partner that may or may not have shown up quite yet. When that person does show up, it will be clear because he or she will honor their values and their boundaries.

Missouri thinks that someone will show up, that I'll meet someone to share the sunshine and grow a garden. If he's out there, and we both come to each other whole, then maybe, just maybe, we'll have a shot at jumping in and managing life, peacefully, together.

COMING HOME

→

On the final day of my road trip adventure, this journey of self-care, I woke up early in a hotel somewhere on the north side of Indianapolis. This was my day to drive home, not to my own home, but to my parents' home in northern Wisconsin. I was driving home to the home I grew up in to spend the day with my family. It was my parents' turn to host our family's annual Christmas in July celebration, except this year it was in August. My brother and I decided to call it Christmas in JulAugust. Our off-season Christmas celebration is everything you'd expect of a December gathering, complete with a Christmas tree and Christmas cookies and Christmas carols and a gift exchange. Relatives come in from multiple states to share this holiday and all of our traditions. I think we all believe that the matriarch of my dad's family, Lorena, is smiling down from up above, happy that the traditions continue down through her great-grandchildren.

As one would expect, upon arriving home for the holiday gathering, I had some interesting conversations with my aunts and uncles and cousins about all of my life's recent changes. They had lots of questions about my book. Evidently, there was a bit of a buzz about this topic for which I wasn't exactly prepared: *"What's it about?"* *"Where were you?"* *"How much more will you travel?"* *"How do you pay for it?"* *"We're proud of you."* *"But where were your kids?"* *"Can't wait to read it."* *"How exciting!"* And, my favorite, *"We will keep praying that you get a real job."* I spent a lot of time smiling and nodding during these conversations, often hiding behind my glass and sipping my drink. My mom must have made a comment about something I was doing because one of my uncles cracked a joke that my mom better be nice to me or she'd end up known as "Chapter Four."

Even though I wasn't exactly prepared, all of these questions and comments were exactly what I needed to hear. As we sang Christmas carols and ate little decorated cookies in the shapes of reindeer and trees, my mind wandered over the last few days, weeks, months. I thought about the experiences and the feelings and what I hoped this book would eventually be. I wished I had been ready for their questions. I was not prepared to pitch my book with a concise elevator speech since it was not even written yet. There's nothing quite like the brutal honesty of your blood relatives to challenge you, support you, and humble you, all in the same conversation.

Truthfully, their congratulatory prodding caused more than a bit of self-doubt. After the gift exchange I hugged my family members and said my goodbyes, saying how great the day was and how I couldn't wait until next year. During my ninety-minute drive back to my home, I asked myself repeatedly what in the actual hell I thought I was doing. The darkness began to wrestle all the light I had felt in the last few days. Why would anyone want to read something I wrote? Who did I think I was? Elizabeth Gilbert? Glennon Doyle? Freaking Oprah?

I was more unsettled on that drive home than I was when I started the journey. The entire plan was to tell the stories of others, but the reality had become something quite different. I had been compelled to focus inward, reliving and processing some of the stories that found me, and many were *about* me. I had been trying to be organic and let the process flow from my heart and soul through my brain and fingers so I could breathe life into words in the hope that they might inspire someone, somewhere ... to be more themselves. To be more authentic. To do more of what they love. To inspire goodness. To be thankful. To connect with others. To share stories in the ways that made the most sense. There is huge risk in sharing some of the darkest pieces of our souls, but only when we share can we learn how we all carry pieces of each other's stories within us.

I remembered the words Peggy shared with me in our first conversation: *Especially as women, we need to learn how to navigate our minds, both the good and the bad, the light and the dark, so that ultimately, we can create acceptance and open our arms and come home to ourselves.*

When we are wrestling our doubts and our word-wounds and our darkness, we need to calm our minds to reduce our fears, to move out of survival mode into a space where we can dream. We need to acknowledge that life is going to be messy; it is never picture perfect as we might imagine it to be. We will live through many series of peaks and valleys in our unique relationships and circumstances. We need to remember that life actually happens in the often silent and unassuming moments that occur when we least expect it. Life happens in the space in between. We need to continue to show up for those moments. We can lose ourselves in times of despair, or we can use those moments to learn who we are and find ourselves. The darkness and the light may wrestle long and hard, but maybe the secret is the resilience and gratitude that's built during the journey. It's only with true gratitude that we can appreciate the peaks, and with the learned practice of resilience that we can manage the pain of the valleys.

While I was driving I had a brief conversation with my daughter, and she could hear the fear and anxiety in my voice. I told her about the questions from my family members. I told her about how many answers I didn't have. Shortly after we hung up, she texted me:

> *Don't be scared. Everyone is offended by something, and not everything can be taken to heart. You've always told me to speak my truth, and this is you speaking yours in the best form possible. I love you mom. <3*

I remembered that this was the girl who told me I had Big Dick Energy. I laughed. Maybe I was doing something right.

During the rest of my drive home I relived with gratitude my memories of the previous weeks' adventures. I recalled the stories that found me. I replayed the conversations with the people I met. I sent vibes of love and gratitude to my framily in North Carolina. I wondered if my new friend had made it to D.C. I treasured up in my heart all the time I had to just live and be free. I decided to unapologetically celebrate my journey, give thanks for my friends and my family, and revel in the conversations that challenged me to find my way home.

About twenty miles outside of my city, I stopped to get gas. When I unbuckled my seat belt, I noticed a fly buzzing about the passenger seat near the window. I opened the window, but I didn't shoo it out. I just smiled as it walked along the seat and then hopped over and walked along the edge where the window slips into the door. I studied the fly as it studied me. I smiled, wondering just how far she had come with me on this adventure. I wondered if she felt that, on this journey, I had found everything I needed to find. I imagined a red ribbon woven throughout each of her delicate wings.

CHAPTER FOUR: MOM

➤———→

This is the part where I want to write about my mom, because in a million ways that are equally different and the same, my mom is my home.

This is the part where I want to explain that my mom, at age seventy-four, hosted about fifty people from around the country for the shenanigans of Christmas in JulAugust, making everyone feel welcome and taken care of. My mom knows how to create a space that feels good for everyone.

This is the part where I want to explain how when I was growing up, my mom's lap was the safest place on earth, how she smelled like contentment and radiated light like an angel. This is the part where I want to say that my mom's beautiful energy could wrap you in a hug from miles away, and also chastise you with her real voice through the written words of a strong, defiant letter. My mom is strong. My mom is a force. My mom is a warrior.

This is the part where I want to share that my mom's courageous spirit of adventure showed up in her youthful undertakings—train rides across the country, a blind date with the man who turned out to be my dad, wearing miniskirts when it was questionable to do so, going away to school when no one else in her family did. Those adventures have inspired each of her kids to look at the world as an open book where we can choose our own paths, write our own pages, and create the journeys to our own destinations.

This is the part where I want to write about how my mom is so fierce, and her love burns so strong, that she faced the darkness of the devil himself, and she won. And even on the days he tries to rise up against her, her love and forgiveness rage back so hard that, even when exhausted, she wins. Those of us who have seen her fierce love and loyalty often sit in silent admiration. We wonder how she maintains her strength.

This is the part where I want to say that when we were children in church, my mom used to "draw our hands" with her own fingertips, tracing the lines of our palms and the outlines of each finger, sending us into trances of silence to hopefully make it quietly through the sermon. When I reciprocated and traced her hand I tried to memorize the shape of her fingers and the feel of her skin. As a child I thought the skin on her hands looked "papery and soft." I always wanted to remember the character of her hands, and I'm glad I did, because sometimes now when I look at my own hands, I think they look like hers. It makes my heart smile.

This is the part where I want to let my mom know that I'm sorry for all the times that I made her worry or made her angry or disappointed her. And this is also the part where I want her to know that I forgive her for the times that she made me worry or made me angry or disappointed me. Because we're humans, and to love is to be vulnerable, and when we're vulnerable we sometimes hurt each other. But in this family we always love and we always forgive, with fierce and unconditional love.

This is the part where I want to say that no matter what happens to our bodies as they age, and our minds as they grow tired, and our souls as they fight to stay alive in these shells made of skin and bones, I will love you forever and ever. Part of our journey here is to learn to navigate life's seasons with grace and with empathy. As you have loved and taken care of me, I promise to love and take care of you.

This is the part where I want to say thank you for being my mom, and for teaching me adventure and bravery and forgiveness and love.

This is the part where I want to say thank you to my mom for always wrapping me in the red ribbons of love, and for teaching me to do the same for my children.

And this is the part where I want to tell you that I love you, Mom, and my love for you will never, ever end.

JESSICA

➤————→

I t takes a great deal of patience and wisdom to turn inward and decide what is really important. It takes conviction and courage to choose to run toward those decisions with reckless abandon.

Moving out of survival mode and into the space to dream can be daunting. Learning to reset boundaries and make decisions within new guardrails is a journey of imperfection, especially in the wake of being jolted into a new reality. As a corporate professional, I was able to spend time in professional development focusing on skills to help others do just that: to define their values and identify obstacles to overcome on the way to their most amazing futures. Over the years I became certified as a coach, as a trainer, as a mediator, and as a change management professional. This served me well in terms of leading teams and facilitating dialogues, and the skills I learned were key in one-on-one coaching relationships.

On one team I managed, a young woman named Jessica asked me to formally take her through the coaching process. I agreed. As we charted the course of her journey, it became clear she had many ideas for her milestones in the coming years, yet her path seemed cloudy. To her, her goals seemed too far away to achieve. We identified what was in the way so she could create meaningful, bite-sized actions to wade through the chaos of life and make sense of her plans.

As with any coaching client, I got excited about her goals right alongside her. As she became energized by her plan and her progress,

I did too. One day when we really mapped out her plan and her timeline, she turned to me and asked, "Where's your timeline? It would be really helpful if I could see your plan because it might give me more ideas and clarity for mine."

Oh shit.

This was the epitome of the pot calling the kettle black. While I was putting on a good game face and doing a pretty good job of navigating my day-to-day life, I had no actual plan for moving out of survival mode and into thriving. I was still in my in between, and I was trying to find the sunshine in life. I certainly wasn't setting boundaries and marking milestones. I was a mess of ideas and wishes and good intent, but I had done nothing in terms of creating an actual vision and plan.

In that moment and with that one question, the tables turned, and Jessica coached me. A light went on as if Glinda the Good Witch whispered over my shoulder, *You've had the power all along, dear.* With a spark of confidence, I took a deep breath and told Jessica that I would begin to work on my formal timeline, and that we could review both our plans during our next session.

The same teacher in high school who leaned down over his podium and would say to me, "You are not stupid!" would say to us, "People don't plan to fail, they only fail to plan." After my divorce—as well as other varying life jolts—my vision for my future was upside down, my plan for living was completely disrupted, and my days felt like absolute chaos. I was floundering. Everything was happening to me instead of me charting my own course ... just like Jessica. The words of a different leader in my life, Tom Goris, Jr., came to mind: *Live your life by design, not by default.* I was reacting and defaulting all over the place. I needed to take some time to reflect and dream and redesign my own life.

I started by spending time journaling and in meditation, sometimes with hot tea, sometimes with a glass of wine, sometimes with candles, and sometimes out in the sunshine. My journal was a small black leather book with gold embossed letters on the front that read, DREAM BIG. Inside those pages I wrote down everything I imagined I wanted, no matter how insignificant or how unrealistic. I wrote down travel goals for me, vacation goals for my kids, financial milestones, the purchases I wanted to make for my home, gifts I wanted to give my family, concerts I wanted to see, and experiences I wanted to have. Nothing was too big or too small; my ideas moved from my soul through my brain to my hands and onto the paper to get organized into buckets of categories that I could eventually sort into a plan.

My next step was adding ages and milestones to build a realistic timeline of events from now until retirement age. When I created my timeline, I planned to retire with my company, but that part of my vision changed with the layoff. As with any major jolt or interruption, I had to reset my vision and start again.

Life lesson: Never be afraid to start again.

After the timeline was charted, I added in my goals. For example, I wanted new kitchen appliances, so I placed that item in the plan where it seemed most appropriate. I also wanted to visit Puerto Rico, so I slotted that milestone where it seemed feasible. I carried on with this exercise until my pages of scribbled ideas were reorganized into a road map that would help guide my journey for the next several years.

A funny thing happens when you chart your course and navigate your life according to your plan. Once you commit to your vision and your plan, the Universe conspires to make it so. In big and small ways, signs show up that move you in the direction of your vision. While you're working to find your life, life begins to find you. Within the first twelve months of having my written plan in place, the appliance store down the road announced its going-out-of-business sale, and I purchased all new kitchen appliances for a fraction of the regular cost. Also, an e-mail came out at work announcing that the women's club annual fall trip would be to San Juan, Puerto Rico. I took it as a sign. I registered for the trip and put my plan into action.

Once I felt my "physical" plan and timeline were both meaningful and relevant to my overall situation, I realized the harder work that I needed to do was the intangible stuff, the work of setting the vision for what I wanted a relationship to look like someday, and to be patient enough to let it find me. It had to look and feel like more than *YES!* typed in a word doc. That took more time, more reflection, and a few more glasses of wine. I went through an exercise to refresh and define my core values. I wrote down what I expected a partnership to actually look like. And I decided that there were some basic pillars (faith, family, home, career, health, legacy) on which I wanted to build my family's future.

This, also, has been a journey of successes and failures. As my life circumstances have changed, I've had to pivot and adjust my goals and milestones. Sometimes I've had to do a hard reset on my beliefs about my end state. Overall, this roadmap renewed my strategy for living, and that strategy has helped me figure out both what I've wanted to say yes and no to for the last several years. It has helped me not only examine but also enforce my boundaries. That process has been and continues to be imperfect, but I've learned to celebrate those imperfections as learning moments while finding life in between. My written plan and framework has helped me release the old to make way for the new. It's moved me down a path that helps me live my life to the fullest and with unapologetic authenticity. *That* is how my healing shows up as I continue to learn to come home to myself.

BLIND DATE

→

When you open yourself up to new beginnings, the Universe often shifts on your behalf. It's a bit of magic meets intention meets opportunity meets luck sprinkled with stardust and maybe a few shakes of holy water. Once you recognize that the Universe has opened up an opportunity specifically for you, it's up to you to either flow, or resist. During my summer journey of healing, the Universe presented me with such an opportunity. Begrudgingly and after much internal debate (resistance), I decided to let go and flow with the offer of a blind date.

This was the second blind date I'd ever been on in my life. After the first one about twenty years ago, I vowed to never do it again. That first one was a favor to my mom to go out with her friend's son who was back from the military. My mom hoped to win her friend's favor and recruit her into our church. At least that's how I remember it. That date did not go well. I think the lady eventually joined my mom's church, but it certainly wasn't because of the date.

This second blind date was a bit different. For me, having lived through the trauma of post-divorce dating and Match.com nonsense and other relationship nightmares, I have had enough. Enough of the boys who claim they are men. Enough of the Republicans claiming to be Independents. Enough of the angry folks claiming they're well-adjusted, and enough of the unannounced, unsolicited dick pics. Seriously. I have spent countless hours in relationship-specific meditation and reflection asking, "What am I supposed to learn from this?" and "What is it about me that is attracting this nonsense into my life?"

The first "relationship" I ventured into after my divorce lasted about three months. I went from elation to devastation at breakneck speed. During that relationship I learned that my heart still felt things. I could still connect with people.

As I opened myself up to the possibility of a relationship, I began to understand more about myself and what I need.

1. I can't date people who don't share my core values, and the truth is that people's values aren't always on display until well into the dating relationship. My good friend once said, "It's nothing until it's six months. At six months it might be something and it might be nothing, but it's nothing until it's six months." Sage advice.

2. I can't date people who want my ovaries and eggs more than they want me.

3. I can't date people who make my kids uncomfortable.

4. I can't date people who have anger management issues which, again, don't always show up until well after the first few months.

5. I can't date people who look at me like I'm a paycheck.

6. I can't date people who just want sex. Physical intimacy is great, but emotional and intellectual intimacy is way more important to me. I believe that if you're lucky enough to find a solid match in the emotional and intellectual space at this point in the game, the physical intimacy is going to be nothing short of spectacular.

7. Finally, and maybe the biggest one, I believe you learn a lot about a person by how they handle conflict. If they blame you for confronting them with evidence about potential indiscretions (like the Craigslist classifieds), there's an issue. At least there is for me. Gaslighting has no place in a true, loving relationship. After all, you have

to learn to resolve your inevitable differences if you're going to walk through the shitstorms of life together.

Several years ago at the direction of a good friend, I made a full list of what I actually wanted in a partner. It's a long list. Some of the items are physical traits (taller than me, doesn't smoke). Some are more about the person's character and what he might love (loves to travel, drinks champagne, etc.). I pulled out that list (written directly under the word *YES!*) and I spent some time reflecting on my post-divorce dating experiences. It didn't take long for me to realize that I'd been making concessions, and over the past several years, I'd been telling myself that it was because the right person who fit all these criteria simply didn't exist. I had convinced myself that I was searching for a unicorn, that no one could possibly fit the tall order that I had created. This was a really convenient way for me to look outward to find excuses, but in the work of healing and self-discovery, the journey inward is where the learning happens. After significant time in reflection and meditation, I came to the painful realization that the problem was me. *I didn't believe that I deserved someone that good in my life.* I had been making concessions because I had not believed myself to be worthy of someone who could match up to the criteria on my list.

Right before my back surgery, I made up my mind that I needed to full-on focus on me and on my healing. I decided this right about the time I realized my surgery was actually a major procedure that required not only significant time to heal but also significant help from family and friends. My focus was not just on physical healing; it was on the emotional stillness required to do the soul work of healing, as well.

During my post-surgery acute healing phase, I learned how to ask for help. I also learned how to set boundaries and say no. I love to say yes to new experiences, meeting new people, helping friends, so learning to say no was hard. However, finally enforcing the boundaries I had set in my mind was incredibly liberating. Those who questioned my need to set boundaries and those who would not honor my boundaries either removed themselves or were promptly removed from my life. Period. I learned to bless and release those people so that I could focus on me.

That's also why I went on my road trip—alone. So I could focus on me and my healing. So I could make the journey out of survival and into "thrival." So I could remember who I was and reclaim who I wanted to be. At some point during my drive to my parents' home for Christmas in JulAugust, something prompted me to go back to some old text messages.

A few months prior, a friend asked me if I'd like to meet his friend. At the time I received the message, I rolled my eyes and put my phone away. I ignored him. I didn't respond. But now, as I drove, I felt less eye-rolly and more open. I thought back to my conversations with Missouri, and I realized that I couldn't possibly meet someone if I didn't bother to even show up. Somewhere in between West Virginia and Indiana I messaged him and said I'd be willing to meet up with this friend. Socially. Since I'd especially recently become more protective of my space, I wanted the three of us to meet out for drinks. Casually. And that he better not be a weirdo. My friend agreed with that approach, reassured me his guy wasn't a weirdo, and arranged a date and time that worked for all three of us. I was kind of dreading it, but I was surprised to realize I was kind of excited about it, too. At least it would be informal and social and safe, and there would be no heavy pressures of a "date."

Of course, my friend bailed at the last minute. *You motherfucker,* I thought to myself. As you've read, my life has had some traumas that put me a bit at odds with the idea of going out alone with a man I'd never met. My friend knew this. While he had reassured me that the man I was meeting was highly reputable and would lose him as a friend if he did anything inappropriate with me, I was still uncertain. He had also taken the time to assure me that this was simply an introduction and not an actual date.

It was totally a date.

On the night of the casual-meeting-turned-date, I arrived fifteen minutes before our designated meeting time, hoping to settle my energy and establish my position at the bar. When I stepped inside, he was already there, having established *his* position at the bar. *Shit!* He must have heard my inner voice yell because he looked up. Our eyes met. He smiled. I smiled back. My hands were a little shaky and my palms were sweaty as I walked over to introduce myself. I think I tried to shake his hand, but he stood up and gave me a hug. I stayed in that hug for a moment too long and breathed him in. He smelled *so good*. His cologne was all I could think about for a minute so I fidgeted with my hands and my chair and my clutch while I got settled. Apparently he arrived at the bar a little early to not only establish his position, but also to research the wine list. When we texted earlier about the fact that it would just be the two of us out for the evening, I had told him I liked New Zealand sauvignon blanc. He had arrived early to see if there was a wine on the list that I would enjoy. I made a mental note that he was thoughtful, and I took that to be a good sign. The owner brought out a flight of wines so we could pick out the flavors best suited to us. We made natural and normal conversation together, even though we had just met a few moments earlier. We sampled the wines and agreed that one, hands down, was superior to the rest. I noted that we had similar taste in wine, which I also took to be a good sign.

The evening turned out to be incredible. The food and the service were spectacular. The chemistry between us was perfect: fun, but not overbearing and not awkward at all. At one point, he joked with our waitress that we were out celebrating our fifteen-year anniversary.

While we chuckled about that and affectionately leaned into each other, our waitress surprised us with two flutes of champagne to celebrate. "Congratulations on fifteen years! Thank you for spending your night with us!"

We laughed more and talked about celebrating our next anniversary with a trip to Thailand. He picked up the tab without me wondering for one second if I should split it or pay, and then he let me wear his jacket when he walked me to my car.

That cologne, though!

I wanted to breathe it in all night. Wearing his jacket with that scent was like being enveloped in complete satisfaction. I can't explain it. I can only feel it. And it was amazing. He was a perfect gentleman. Not once did I feel unsafe or afraid. As far as dates go, this one was, hands down, the best.

After the blind date, I found myself in a particularly happy mood, thinking about how well that night went. This man had not flinched at me being divorced with three kids. He didn't shy away when I told him I had just had a major surgery, and he didn't cut and run when he found out I had just been laid off. Maybe most importantly, he didn't think I was nuts for writing a book. On the contrary, he told me he thought I was intelligent. Fun. Good to talk with. That I had nice eyes. That I had a great smile. That I impressed him. At the end of the night, he told me I was beautiful. Maybe it was the wine, his cologne, or how he looked at me, or maybe it was a combination of all of those things, but I decided that I believed him.

It occurred to me that when you date in your early twenties—maybe your thirties—you are likely looking for someone to build a life with. I see so many "Happy anniversary, honey" posts on Facebook that showcase couplehood and happiness. They've made it through the chaos and adventure of life, raising kids together, seeing them through school, sharing a home for all these years ... That is awesome and I love seeing my friends celebrate these milestones. I appreciate it when they post their loving, congratulatory messages with brutal honesty about the fact that life isn't easy and that somehow they've survived it together. But some of us haven't made it, and there's no shame in that. Our marriages have failed, and we've had to find meaning in a life on our own. Suddenly, here in my forties, I'm less concerned about *building* a life with someone, and I'm more concerned about *sharing* a life with someone. I want someone who looks at life as an adventure, not someone who looks at me as a destination. There is a world to see and experiences to share, and it would be so incredible to weather the storms and the sunshine of life with a best friend, a lover, a partner.

Our first blind date led to more, and things have actually been pretty incredible. Who knows where this will lead? After meeting him, I reviewed my list of criteria for a potential partner, that list I created about four years ago. Based on our conversations so far, my blind date seems to check all the boxes:

- A nonsmoker.
- Has no criminal record.
- Is taller than me.
- Is intelligent.
- Is gainfully employed.
- Has a good sense of humor.
- Doesn't want more kids.
- Provides love and patience and lots of laughter.
- Is my best friend.
- Is a partner who wants to run a household and build a life and leave a legacy someday.
- Has patience and a desire to merge and manage the craziness of real life.
- Looks at the world like it's an adventure waiting to happen and is willing to explore it with me.
- Likes Champagne.
- Self-confident rather than arrogant.
- Trustworthy.
- Holds himself accountable.
- Likes lots of music, preferably live.
- Shares similar values (loyalty, integrity, balance, unconditional positive regard).
- Is slow to anger.
- Will get dressed up and surprise me and take me out.
- Wakes up and actively chooses me every single day ... and is someone I choose, too.
- Wants to show up together and leave together and go to bed together every day.
- Will never stop dating me.
- Has good oral hygiene.

- Will take selfies or make sure we have pictures of us and isn't afraid to share that we're together.
- Is not critical of mistakes (mine or his) but is always willing to learn together.
- Is philanthropic.
- Is not a Jesus freak.
- Believes in karma and good energy.
- Is compassionate.
- Can communicate. As long as there is true dialogue, there is a relationship.
- Is a good example for my kids, who will show my boys how to be true gentlemen, and who will set the standard for my daughter.
- Shows up and participates in life (and in my kids' lives).
- Will create new traditions with me and my kids.
- Sees the glass as half full, unless we drink it and need to refill it.
- Will look at me when I'm eighty like it's still the very first time he's truly seeing me.
- Will holds hands.
- Swears appropriately and grammatically correctly.
- Kisses me under the mistletoe.
- Brings the mistletoe to make the magic happen.
- Will work out but not live only for the gym.
- Knows the difference between BBC and FOX News, and who prefers BBC wholeheartedly.
- Provides unconditional love, the kind that gets you through the messy days without being cruel.
- Will be honored to wear a wedding ring and will refuse to take it off.
- Will take the high road and encourage me to do the same.

This is not the description of a unicorn. This is the description of the person who is right for me. And it took me a long time to say it, but *I'm worthy*. Does that make me arrogant or selfish for feeling that way? Absolutely not. It's the gift of wisdom that comes with time and healing and setting boundaries. Not just saying but fully knowing I'm worthy is a remarkable step in this journey of healing, so I'm going to pause, and I'm going to invite Happiness to celebrate with me. This is a major milestone as I'm finding my way in the adventure of life.

Part of me wishes I would have learned some of my life's lessons and walked intentionally down this path of healing sooner, but had the timing been different maybe some of the people and the moments I treasure most wouldn't be a part of my story. Perhaps the Universe lined up these life events in wisdom. To wish away any parts of my journey would be to wish away lessons learned, and those lessons would have come around one way or another at some point anyway. Maybe, if things had unfolded any differently, my blind date wouldn't have happened, and maybe I never would have smelled that cologne and felt that overwhelming sense of comfort when I breathed him in that first time. Perhaps I wouldn't be ready to stand in my own power and say, *I'm whole. I'm worthy. I'm ready.*

Regardless of what lessons and milestones the Universe has in store next, I'm celebrating the courage it took to get to this point. I'm celebrating the soul work and inner healing that brought me here, to this place, today. I'm paddling down the river of life at the pace my body can handle, and I'm focused on the never-ending journey of learning and growth. I'm releasing the pressures of expectation and unapologetically living my own authentic life. I'm taking time daily to breathe in the light of patience and gratitude, and I'm consciously making decisions that help me savor each moment. Most importantly, I'm wrapping red ribbons of love around my sons and my daughter and throughout my ever-evolving tribe.

Perhaps the long journey home to ourselves is actually a celebration of finding an extraordinary life … in between. My hope is that you reimagine your wildest dreams, open your arms, and welcome yourself home. There's wisdom and peace and magic in the beautifully imperfect, authentic story of you.

4

TRAVEL NOTES

"The secret of change is to focus all of your energy, not on fighting the old, but on building the new."

—SOCRATES

JOURNAL PROMPTS

➤———→

L ife, in all its beautiful imperfection, will always present us with something to overcome. "Arrival" at some final destination where everything is perfect is nothing but a fleeting moment, one of the peaks in the mountain range of life. The peaks are inevitably followed by some type of decline, and the pattern of ups and downs continues indefinitely. There is no permanent state of sun-kissed and semi-charmed, but there is the magic of finding life in between those peaks and valleys. We can only do our journey's soul work when we turn inward and learn the lessons the Universe is offering us.

Please use these questions as a starting point to reflect and begin that journey home to yourself.

1. Describe a jolt that you've experienced in your life, personally and/or professionally.

2. If you chose to discuss that jolt with anyone, how did you approach the conversation? If you chose to not discuss that jolt, write it down as if you're discussing it with a friend.

3. Write about a time you've felt cared for.

4. How did you or how can you express gratitude for those who've cared for you?

5. Who are the three or four people you admire most?

    a. What traits do they embody?

    b.   Why are those traits important to you?

    c.   Do they remind you of someone or of a specific event or time?

    d.   If you could share one thing with each of those individuals, what would you say?

6.   Pause to take an inventory of what is happening in your current life. What is on your calendar today or this week?

    a.   What about that is most overwhelming to you?

    b.   When you pause to consider your current situation, what are the three things you're most thankful for?

7.   Say this out loud after filling in the blank: "I forgive myself for: _____."

8.   Say this out loud after filling in the blank. "I forgive _____ for _____."

9.   If/when you have negative thoughts in darkness, what will you focus on to bring in the light?

10. For you personally, name the items that fall into the buckets of self-maintenance vs. self-care.

11. When you think of your future life partner, that person is or looks like/feels like ...

12. List the things/experiences you desire in the respective timeframes:

    a.   0–12 months

    b.   1–3 years

    c.   3–5 years

    d.   5–10 years

    e.   10+ years

13. List the beliefs, people, or situations that are getting in the way of going after what you desire, or of living your most authentic life.

a. In an ideal world, how would you choose to address these beliefs, people, or situations?

14. Fill in the blank and then say this out loud: "I promise to love and honor myself and my space by committing to/ doing the following:_____."

AFTERWORD: TEAR OUT

➤———→

Tear this page out. Put it in your purse. Hang it on your mirror.
Give it to a friend. Add to it. Make it your own.

You. Are. Worthy.

Fall in love with the journey of falling in love with yourself.

Find your tribe. Hold them close.
And the ones who aren't your tribe—let them go.

Speak to yourself with the same compassion
that you would to others.

Honor your boundaries. Examine how it feels when others do not.

Allow dark thoughts to serve their purpose. Learn from them, then
turn them over to the light.

Ask for help. Specifically. And when you can, offer help.
Specifically.

Look for the red ribbons that bind us all together;
we are all connected.

At the end of each day, open your arms
and welcome yourself home.

Savor every moment, not just the destinations.
Find your life, in between.

ACKNOWLEDGMENTS

Thank you for reading. Thank you for listening to my story. I hope it inspires you to think about your own story. I'm deeply grateful for every person who had a hand in this book coming to life, whether we shared a conversation, an adventure, a bottle of wine, or just a smile in passing.

To Carrie Severson, owner of The Unapologetic Voice House: Thank you for taking a chance on me, for believing in my idea, for helping me navigate this journey, in all the ways. I appreciate you nurturing my unconventional approach. Most of all, thank you for inspiring me to stand in my power.

To Jess, my editor: Thank you for making the process of reviewing my soul as painless as possible, for your patience, and for your humor. Thank you for helping me believe that my story is worth telling.

To Meredith, the cover designer: Thank you for creating visual order out of the passionate chaos of my ideas.

To Candy Barone: Thank you for gently nudging me toward this project over the last several years. Thank you for showing me the things in myself that without you I could not see. Thank you for your passion. Your friendship is one of the reasons my spirit is free.

A special group shout-out to Jacy, Bernadette, Yvonne, Paula, Kate, Mikenzie, Grace, Amy, Corie, Sydney, and Jessica: Thank you for providing your thoughts and feedback on the words of these pages and talking through how they might actually come alive. Thank you for your gentleness, honesty and encouragement. I am so very grateful.

To Jen Buccholz and Rhonda Noordyk: Thank you for helping create the connections that moved this book out of my imagination and into reality. I will be forever grateful for your inspiration in this work of heart.

To Brett and Lisa (Tanya), Hannah, and Nolan: Thank you for being there when I didn't know I needed you. Thank you for your unconditional friendship. Thank you for being my framily. Tanya and Gail are due for drinks!

To Peggy: Thank you for sharing your spirit with mine. Thank you for pouring your energy into me for protection and healing. Thank you for joining me on my long journey home.

To Heidi and Todd: Thank you for inviting me on the canoe trip and making me part of your tribe. There's no group I'd rather face the storms with!

To Kate: Thank you for spontaneously adventuring with me and becoming part of my tribe. No matter our distance I hold you in red ribbons. I can't wait for the screenplay.

To the Wisconsin Humane Society: Thank you for Coco. She rescued me when I didn't know I needed saving.

To Rebecca and Noel: Thank you for Charlie Girl and T-Rex. Charlie is the gift that keeps on giving, and Rexy completes all of us in a way we didn't expect. We are so grateful for you!

To Linda B. and Dianne L.: Thank you for listening to me and for helping me make sense of my being. Thank you for encouraging me to walk into the fire so that I could continue my healing.

To Jessica: Thank you for flipping the coaching script on me and forcing me to practice what I preach! Thank you also for handing tissues over our shared cubicle wall when you heard me crying. I'm grateful for you!

To Moby: Thank you for choosing me. Thank you for being consistently and equally present and crazy when that is exactly what I need to navigate my in between space. I am so grateful for our standing margarita dates and for the ridiculous amounts of guac we consumed together. Thank you for letting me cry in your lap, without shame, when I just needed to cry. You've inspired me to be better and do better. I'm lucky to call you friend.

To the Shevil Knevils, past and present: Thank you for teaching me to get up every time I got knocked down. Thank you for giving me the sisterhood I didn't know I needed. Thank you for all the memories we've made together, and all the memories we have yet to create. Thank you for the best locker room talks and the best locker room fridge in the history of ever. *Never Say Die!*

To Ze: You are my person. Thank you for carrying me when I could not walk. I am eternally grateful you reminded me that there really was sunshine when all I could feel was the rain. And, we're pretty.

To Norma: Thank you for sharing your tent, your air mattress, your blanket, your food, your encouragement, your friendship. I will never forget that "an organized bench is an intimidating bench." NSD!

To Paula: Thank you for all of the conversations that have prompted reflection and healing. Thank you for being willing to go to those dark places with me so that we could also come out and walk in the light, together. (Queue music: "I'm So Fancy"!)

To Yvonne: Thank you for being my ride or die, for sharing your wisdom and perspective and grace in so many of life's situations. I am a better person because I am privileged enough to call you friend.

To Bernadette: Thank you for being the other half of my change management brain. Collaborating with you professionally was one of the highlights of my corporate career. Thank you for your presence and your calm. Thank you for reading the pages of this book when it was a first draft filled with questions and ideas and for providing honest feedback. Thank you for being a kindred spirit on our journey through this life.

To Mikenzie and Lauren: Thank you for being my goddess daughters. Promise me, but more importantly, promise yourselves, that you will find the inspiration and courage to always choose authenticity on your magical journeys of life.

To Kirsty: I am grateful for your friendship and love and your sense of unbridled adventure. Thank you for giving me a second home across the pond. From 1999 to 2016 to today and to forever: *You haven't changed a fucking bit!*

To Lora, Angie, and Tom: I am so thankful for your unwavering friendship and for all of the laughs and adventures we've been having since 1997. In a lot of ways, we found each other when we were "in between." Hell, in a lot of ways we're still living in between! I'll be forever grateful that the Universe brought us together.

To my Blind Date: Thank you for being a part of my journey and for cheering me on in this process. Thank you for recognizing the importance of honoring boundaries. I'm so happy we chose to hold a safe place for each other. Cheers to another fifteen years!

To Jacy: You are my best friend and my sister wife. You are the peanut butter to my jelly. Thank you for drawing hearts in my peanut butter sandwiches and for straining my orange juice! I mean it sincerely when I say I couldn't do life without you.

To my mom and my dad: Thank you for being the role models that you are, for teaching all of us kids the importance of hard work and unconditional love. Thank you for giving us a home filled with music. Thank you for your patience and for trying to understand that I don't fit into the box of life I originally came in. Thank you for making sure we knew how to swim. Thank you for being a safe place when I swam out too far in the deep waters. Thank you for wrapping our whole family in the red ribbons of your love.

To my siblings and their partners, Corie and Todd, Eric and Linda, Andrew and Naomi: Thank you for binding our family together with each of your strengths, so we can celebrate all of our differences. Corie, thank you for paving the way with patience and grace. Eric, thank you for teaching me how to throw a ball and shoot a basketball, and to always leave the court/field on a good hit or a made shot. Andrew, thank you for letting me sing with you and for the times when you helped me find the music. And Linda, even though you're an outlaw, thank you for keeping us all in good hairstyles and for covering up the gray!

To my children, Sydney, Micah, and Camden: Thank you for your patience and your understanding while I figured out who I am as a mom and who I am as a whole person. I am so happy your souls chose to go on this life journey with mine. I wish for you the lessons you need to learn and the patience to learn them, and my hope is that each of you chooses to show up authentically, because you are magical just the way you are. I hope you look back at our lives together with love, and that you tell your kids the beautifully imperfect stories of us. My red ribbons are wrapped tightly around you, and they will be forever. I love you more.

ABOUT THE AUTHOR

⇒———→

CANDY LEIGH lives in Southeastern Wisconsin and is the president and owner of Candy Leigh Coaching, LLC. She spent the majority of her career in the financial services industry for a Fortune 500 company, most notably developing diversity and inclusion leadership programs and also consulting for sales executives and leaders across the nation. After a successful corporate career she decided to branch out on her own to pursue her dream of writing and consulting with individuals, encouraging all people to stand in their truth and create their own narratives. Candy believes that when we can honestly share our authentic selves in safe spaces, not only do we show up as better employees/spouses/partners, we ultimately open ourselves up to leading more fulfilling lives. Her personal mission is to help and motivate womxn to stand in their truth and live authentic lives.

After growing up in Manitowoc, Wisconsin, Candy completed her undergraduate degree in public relations and organizational communication at the University of Wisconsin–La Crosse. She went on to receive her master of arts in communication from the University of Wisconsin–Milwaukee, where she taught interpersonal communication and studied cultural communication with a focus on gender identity and conflict resolution. She is a certified coach and a certified trainer, and also holds certifications in mediation and negotiation and change management. She is the mother of three children and two long-haired miniature dachshunds, Charlie Girl and T-Rex. When she is not with her family, she is often traveling to visit her "framily" (friends who are family) around the United States and in England. Candy is a retired rollergirl, former triathlete and half-marathoner, avid yoga enthusiast, Double Stuff Oreo lover, and self-proclaimed goddess of her own untamed and beautifully imperfect life.

Made in the USA
Columbia, SC
05 December 2020

26416922R00107